From

T R KIRBY

NO 4 RALEIGH COURT.

NOT THE PURSER'S DAUGHTER?

NOT THE PURSER'S DAUGHTER?

A Memoir

Volume Two

Jill Ashley Miller

STRATHMORE PUBLISHING

LONDON

2008

First published in Great Britain by Strathmore Publishing,
41 Kingsway Place, Sans Walk, London ECIR 0LU, 2008

Design and origination by David McLean, London
Typeset in Manticore

Edited by Christopher Pick

ISBN 978-0-9550887-6-6

Printed and bound by Portland Print, Kettering NN16 8UN

All the proceeds from this volume will be given to Norwich Mencap to create
an amenity fund for my Down's Syndrome daughter Catherine and her friends
George and Lennie. They moved in autumn 2008 to a 'Supported Living'
bungalow after living in their residential home, Burlingham House, for almost
thirty years. This fund will provide extras, for example plants for the garden
and taxis for trips to outside events such as Gateway clubs and the pantomime.

JAM

This book has been privately printed. Further copies may be obtained from
Mark Ashley Miller of The Present Finder Ltd, Unit 1, South Western Business
Park, Sherborne DT9 3PS (01935 815195) by letter or telephone; or by
email, info@thepresentfinder.co.uk ; or from his website,
www.thepresentfinder.co.uk. All proceeds will be passed to Norwich Mencap.

Frontispiece: Pastel by Ernest Sichel of Jill Ashley Miller aged five (see page 20).

Contents

To Margaret Evelyn McNaughton.
Killed whilst bicycling by a Devon-General bus
at Battens Corner, Helberton. Devon.
August 14th 1940.

We are now approaching Jaa's country.
Does your gay spirit still wander down that
                                        Devon lane
Reliving what once was, and perhaps what might
                                        have been
As I've so often done?
Can you remember Jaa, the carefree happiness
        of heart we felt,
The laughter with no hint of pain
Which was to fall so soon from the already
                                        darkening sky?
A stranger, unannounced as is Death's wont
Came suddenly within our midst, to terrify,
And we could only guess that you must die.

Can it be seven years since you were torn away
How vivid still that August day!
But in the years between
Despite the sorrow and the aching emptiness of
                                        heart
(We missed you so - the gap has not been filled
We have not forgotten you my Jaa.
Your clothes have not been laid apart
As plucked petals from a living flower wither
                                        and fade
No name unspoken, chilling suddenly on lips
That are afraid to bring yourself to mind.
But we have kept your flame alive within our
                                        hearts,
Tending it jealously from fiercer winds
That if one day you should by chance return
You need not fear that anything is changed
Or your dear self forgotten -
How could that be?

                        Paddington to Kingsbridge. Aug 7.4

My manuscript 'fair copy' of the poem I wrote in memory of my sister, seven years after her death (see also page 87).

6

In abiding memory of my beloved sister,
Margaret Evelyn McNaughton,
snatched from us so cruelly on 14 August 1940,
aged just thirteen.

This volume is a gift of love to salute her bright spirit.
Her death changed my life for ever.

Peggy riding in Birchington gymkhana, August 1939, aged twelve.

Preface

This book, *Not the Purser's Daughter?*, is the second in the trilogy of my family memoir. The first volume, *Call Back Yesterday*, described the history of my father's and mother's families, the McNaughtons and the Kitsons, from 1685 until 1925. This one takes us from my Yorkshire birth in 1925 to 1946 and my demobilisation from the Wrens after the end of the Second World War.

The title needs some explanation. As related in chapter two, my father and I had no rapport whatsoever, and I often question my paternity. My mother, trapped in an arid marriage, had several lovers, one of whom was the purser of the cruise ship in which they sailed to the Canaries in 1925. If you look at the photograph on page 17 you will understand why I hope he was not my father. However, as Lord Melbourne famously declared, 'Who the devil can tell who's anybody's father?'

Because Stewart, my father's brother, married Enid, my mother's sister, I was blessed with double cousins, Ronald, Margaret and Alison, whose photograph will be found on page 63. After the war, when we were both grown up, Margaret, who was the same age as Peggy, became as close to me as a sister. If I am spared, volume three will describe our life together in Cambridge, my visit to her in Burma after her marriage to a soldier, my recruitment there by MI6 and my own marriage in 1956.

This book would not have been possible without the help of my cousins in the UK and in Australia who have given me photographs, information, anecdotes and gossip. The family tree prepared by Donald McNaughton, my second cousin, has been an invaluable tool in my research, and Dr David Boswell enabled me to find out more about my great-grandfather's second wife, Mary Laura Fisher Smith. If there is anyone else whom I have failed to thank, I apologise.

The illustrations come from private collections, with the exception of those on pages 24 and 140 which are reproduced with the permission of *The Times*. If any acknowledgement has been omitted, I apologise.

Once again, the shape of this book is entirely due to the brilliance of two people, my designer and my editor, David McLean and Christopher Pick, who between them have transformed a rustic effort into the pretty thing you see today.

JILL ASHLEY MILLER
Beccles, Autumn 2008

Wren watchkeepers at Lowestoft, April 1946. The author is second on the left.

Enid McNaughton, aged twenty-seven, and her son Ronald, about eight months, 1925.

Chapter 1

Genesis

'From whence we had our being and our birth'

Pericles 1.2.114

'Pull,' yells the midwife, 'Pull, pull hard.'

It is a dank afternoon in mid-November. A young woman, her hair matted with sweat, lies on the bed. As each agonising pain moves to a swelling crescendo, she tugs, as instructed, on the sheet knotted to the rail above her head.

This is her third confinement. She has already lost two sons, the first, inexplicably, at three months old – a so-called 'cot death'. She recalls the terrible day when, looking after him on the nurse's day off, she went outside to find him lifeless in his pram. Later, Dr Hall gently told the stricken parents that their son had been born with an enlarged thymus gland, affecting his lymphatic system, and that his heart had stopped.[1] The following year, pregnant again, she slipped, carrying a heavy vase. The red-haired son born three months later had spina bifida. An operation the next day was of no avail. Later, Mr Harris, the surgeon, explained that, as well as the damaged spine, the baby had been born with hydrocephalus (water on the brain) and was having fits. He was unlikely to survive. In the event, he lingered for six weeks, dying in the nursing home on 19 March. The next day, for the second time in less than two years, the grieving father registered his dead son.[2] The young woman recalls her father's harsh words, which continue to taunt her: 'You and Jack don't seem very good at having children, you'd better not have any more.'

She is determined that, despite her father's gloom and her husband's indifference, this child will live to comfort her old age.

Her painful reverie is pierced by the midwife's cry. Through the

My grandfather, the Reverend G. F. A. McNaughton, aged about sixty.

haze of ether she hears not 'Pull' but 'Push, push hard.' After a few minutes, a head emerges. 'It's a girl, you have a little daughter.'

It is 18 November 1925. I am born.

* * *

'What shall we call her'? My father, who loved Robert Louis Stevenson, suggested the heroine of one of his favourite books – Catriona. 'No one will know how to pronounce it,' countered my mother, correctly. Jack tried again, 'What about Rhona or Rhoda?' He was determined to have something Scottish. My mother demurred. Suddenly, her face lit up – 'I know, we will call her Jill.' And so, thanks to the vapid verse of an old nursery rhyme, I was saddled with this prosaic name.

Thankfully, they decided to put Catherine, the name of one of my godmothers, in front of the dreary Jill. If only they had chosen Emily, after my second godmother, I should not have been so displeased in later life. They did not know that this child would have a penchant for royalty and would spend years practising her signature with a noble flourish. Catherine has a regal tone, but whoever has heard of a Princess Jill? It sounds like someone in a pantomime.

Jill McNaughton (the author) aged about six months, 1926.

And so it was that, on 25 January 1926, my saintly grandfather, the Reverend

George McNaughton, baptised me, 'according to the forms of the Church of Scotland', in the drawing-room of Longwood, my parents' home. Although my grandfather signed his name with 'a' as the second letter, it appears as 'McNaughton' on my birth certificate – presumably my father left it out so as to save time and to annoy his father. My godmothers were two great-aunts: Catherine Gray, my father's mother's sister, and Emily Kitson, my mother's formidable aunt. Aunt Kate tried to persuade my parents to spell my first name with a 'K' rather than with 'C', which she hated. I am glad they demurred.[3] My other godmother, Emily, was now an old woman living in lonely splendour in a vast house in Tunbridge Wells. My godfather was Uncle 'Jumbo', a business associate of my father of whom I never heard again. Thus were my spiritual needs provided for.

My grandfather, baptising me, poured the Holy Water on to my forehead,[4] smoothing away a lock of hair as he did so. 'A woman's forehead is the finest feature in her face,' he declared, 'never cover it with a fringe.' He sent up a silent prayer that this child would survive.

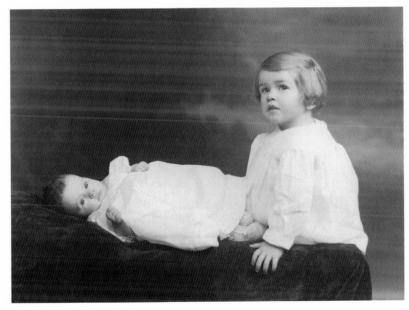

Jill McNaughton aged about two with her infant sister Peggy, about three months, autumn 1927.

I was his second grandchild, following Ronald, who was born to Stewart, my father's brother, and Enid in February 1925. My mother's parents now had seven: Jane Nevett, born in Australia in 1920, followed by her sister, Doris, in 1922 and their brother, Chester, in 1925; John Shiell, Violet's son, in 1922; Joyce Harris in 1924; Ronald McNaughton in 1925; and, finally, me.

* * *

Longwood, where I spent the first five years of my life, lay on the edge of the village of Shadwell, about four miles north of Leeds. It was a solid house, built of Yorkshire stone and set on a terrace reached by four or five steps. The grounds, mainly of lawn, were surrounded by a dry-stone wall dividing the garden from the road beyond. To the back of the house was a cobbled yard surrounded by stables, and it was here that my father cranked his Alvis each morning before driving to work. Now I crank the cogs of memory to recall those distant days.

I am about two years old and have been put outside in my pram while Nanny has a well-earned rest. I am a lively child and jig up and down, secured by the harness which attaches me to the pram. Suddenly, without warning, I am upside down on the cobbles. My right hand hits the ground; the nail on the middle finger bears witness to this day. My screams are heard by Calvert, the gardener, who comes running to pick me up.

It was at about this time that my sister was born. Although my parents had only been married for nine years, they were already bored with each other. The vivacity that had once so enchanted my father had long ago disappeared. But my mother was determined that I should not be an only child, and she used all her wiles to revive the flagging interest of her husband. Her perseverance was rewarded, and on 24 July 1927 my sister was born.

My father was determined that this child should be called after his beloved mother, Margaret. But his sister-in-law Enid, Stewart's wife, was also pregnant, and both brothers wished to bag the name. Enid was three months ahead, and on 1 April 1927 she proudly presented her husband with a daughter whom they called

Margaret. Jack, not to be outdone, chose the same name, but, to differentiate, shortened it to Peggy, an abbreviation she hated.

Peggy is much admired. She has auburn curls, like her Kitson grandfather. When we go to stay in his large London house, there is much crooning over her pram. 'Isn't she lovely,' sigh the servants as they gaze upon her. Left alone in the room for a moment, I feel the pangs of jealousy. No one is taking any notice of me. I will dig out the eyes of this creature who has come to steal my thunder. Fortunately, Nanny returns and I am told that I am 'a horrid little girl'. It is difficult to explain that I only want a little attention too, but no one understands. I am not yet two years old.

My father never shed his Calvinistic distaste for the body, despite ten years of marriage. One day, when I was about three years old, I wandered into my parents' bedroom, where they no longer shared a bed. He was in his pyjama top. Highly embarrassed, he shooed me from the room and I was told not to come back. The chamber pot was returned to the po cupboard for the housemaid to empty later.

As she grew older, my sister became an enchanting companion. In the garden were the remains of old pigsties. We pretended we were piglets and called each other 'Yeye-yeye'. Although the house was so near Leeds, the woods were alive with sounds of doves and sometimes we found a hedgehog.

The maternity nurse, Nurse Bagnall, was replaced by a fresh-faced girl from London, Ena Kett, whom we called 'Nanny'. On fine afternoons she took us to walk in Roundhay Park, a few minutes away. Here, in the deep chasms, were narrow paths beside rushing streams. We walked carefully. It was slippery on the mossy stones and it would be easy to fall in. Rogie, our lively black Aberdeen terrier, dashed about, barking furiously.

As you climbed the terrace steps and entered the house, our nursery was on the right. Among the furniture were elm ladder-back chairs, one of which I still possess. Here Peggy and I had our meals looking out across the lawn to the dry-stone wall beyond. Bowling along the road (today the busy A6120) were new-fangled monsters, double-decker buses. They were a welcome sight to the maids, May and Lucy Smith, two sisters from Hull. On their weekly half-day off, they would escape to the bright lights of the city where 'talking pictures' had just arrived. The next day they would tell Nanny about the glamorous Ronald Colman, the handsome Douglas Fairbanks and the lovely Mary Pickford.

In the corner of the nursery stood a white triangular cupboard which fitted neatly into the space. It was built in two halves, one of top of the other. One day, two boy cousins, Ian and Nigel Kitson,[5] come to tea. Nigel is about my age, Ian two years older. Jigging about, as boys do, they dislodge the cupboard and the top half comes crashing down upon their heads. There is much twittering from the nannies, but no one is hurt.

In the hall stood a grandfather clock, made by Peter Miller of Alloa, which continues to tick in my own hall today. Beside it was the red embroidered chair, with lion's claw feet, now in my attic. To the left of the hall was the drawing-room. It was here that I made the first important discovery of my life. My grandfather McNaughton, now retired from his living in Carsphairn, Galloway, had given his elder son two breakfront bookcases and his fine library. One of these had four pull-down cupboards, easily reached by a four-year-old. Inside, I find a volume describing Queen Victoria's diamond jubilee and am instantly hooked. The handsome coloured frontispiece depicts the nineteen-year-old Queen in her coronation robes, and I think to myself that she looks very like my mother's friend Lettice Fox. Thus I begin on my life-long love-affair with royalty.

One day, my mother suggested that we go to visit old Martha, one of the housemaids from her parents' home, now living in Dewsbury, a few miles from Leeds. To our great delight, we boarded a tram and walked up the steep cobbled street to Martha's small house, a typical back-to-back. My mother was greeted warmly – a visit by 'Miss Doris' was an occasion. The iron kettle steamed on the black-leaded hob. On the floor was a rug made of multi-coloured rags. Peggy and I were fascinated.

My mother's view of sex was as far removed from my father's as possible. This is probably the reason they were so incompatible.

For a woman of her day and upbringing she was remarkably free of inhibition. Talking about sex did not embarrass her. I must have been about four years old and returning from a walk in Roundhay Park when I decided to ask her something that had been bothering me: 'Where did I come from?' She is always truthful about such things and tells me, in a matter-of-fact way, how hens lay eggs and how chickens emerge from them. I absorb this information. A few days later, Peggy and I are taken by Nanny to the birthday party of a neighbour, Rosemary Pickersgill, a well-brought up child of my own age. Her parents live in a large house, approached from the lodge gates by a long uphill drive. It is a formal party; the little girls are in party dresses and velvet cloaks, the boys in frilly shirts and short velvet trousers. In the middle of tea, I decide to impart my new-found knowledge. I am a precocious child and know that this hand grenade I am about to lob, during a lull in the conversation, will cause chaos. My small voice pipes up: 'Mummy got us from the hens.' There is a stunned silence and then all the nannies start talking at once. They do not want their charges contaminated by this vulgar little girl. All their babies were found at the bottom of the garden, under gooseberry bushes.

Sometimes my parents disappeared for long holidays. When I was about four they departed for six weeks to the Canary Islands. My mother was anxious that we should be well looked after and engaged Nurse Tunnicliffe, who had excellent references from St

My mother arm-in-arm with the purser of my parents' cruise ship to the Canaries, c 1925. Can this lugubrious-looking man really be my father? I hope not.

Jack flirting on a cruise *c* 1929, while his wife looks on.

Thomas' Hospital. During their absence, we went to stay with Aunt Nell,[6] who was married to A.K. Wolfe-Barry, an eminent engineer and the son of Sir John Wolfe-Barry, engineer of Tower Bridge.[7] They lived in a handsome house on Chelsea Embankment. Nell noticed that her two nieces looked thin and had poor appetites. In the parlance of the day, we were 'peaky'. On my mother's return, she told of her concern. One evening, on Nurse Tunnicliffe's day off, I remembered something important as we went to bed. 'Oh, Mummy, you've forgotten our syrup of figs.' 'What do you mean? You don't need it.' 'Oh, but we always have it, Nurse gives us a tablespoon every night.' My mother was horrified and Tunnicliffe was sacked on the spot. The following morning, and I still remember it (as I still remember the disgusting taste of the syrup of figs), she stood at the top of the terrace and uttered this malediction: 'One more step on the Road to the Cross'.

My father Jack McNaughton in his Alvis, with Jill (aged four) and Peggy (two) in the dickey-seat, *c* 1929.

In the summer of 1929 we drove to Filey for our seaside holiday. My parents sat in the front of the Alvis while my sister and I were in the dickey seat behind. There was no

Christmas tableau at my first school, Mrs Johns', Leeds, Christmas 1930. I am in the centre of the front row; Peggy is at the right end of the same row, wearing wings.

sense of danger as the wind ruffled our hair – only excitement. Seat belts did not exist but miraculously we did not fall out. We stayed at a small boarding-house where we found our cousins, Ronald and Margaret McNaughton, with their Nanny, Winnie. At a beach shop nearby we bought buckets, spades, multicoloured windmills on a stick and paper flags to fly on top of our sandcastles. The rubber lining of my waders had a sandy smell and the gulls cried overhead.

I was now four and it was time to go to school. My mother's friend Mary Pickersgill sent her daughter Rosemary to Mrs Johns, who ran a small dame school in Leeds. I joined her there. But my first morning was not propitious. A rough boy tried to grab a book I was reading, so I socked him. He retaliated and two yelling children, both with bloody noses, were sent home in disgrace.

Some of our neighbours, who lived in grand houses, gave smart birthday parties for their children – there was an element of 'keeping up with the Jones's'. For some reason, our usual nursery lunch before such events was tripe and onions, which I could not bear. I was invariably sick. At one such party I was left alone and yelled to be taken home. My mother was sent for. I was not invited to choose a present from the bran tub as I left, and felt aggrieved.

During the autumn of 1930, my mother decided that I should be painted. We visited the studio of Ernest Sichel, a well-known local artist, and I was told to sit very still. The pastel portrait he produced shows a serious small girl with wide hazel eyes, who looks upon the world with interest and curiosity. Two copies were made – the second for my godmother Emily, who, it was hoped, would be moved to bestow some of her large fortune upon her goddaughter. Nothing was forthcoming beyond a terse note of thanks.

In November, when I became five, Great-Aunt Nellie[8] took me to the theatre to see *Peter Pan* for my birthday treat. She was a lovely old lady, about seventy years old, and she wore a narrow black velvet band round her throat. On her chin was a large, hairy mole. It is my first visit to a theatre and 'The Grand' does not disappoint. Built in 1878, in the heyday of Victorian building fever, it is a

Grandchildren with Nanny Goff at Number 3 Cadogan Square, December 1928. In the back row are Joyce Harris, Thelma's daughter; Jill McNaughton; Nanny holding Stephen Goff, Angela's son; Jane Nevett, Evelyn's daughter, holding Peggy McNaughton; and John Shiell, Violet's son. Seated are Margaret McNaughton, Enid's daughter; Cynthia Shiell, Violet's daughter; Anne Nevett, Evelyn's daughter; Beryl Harris, Thelma's daughter; and Ronald McNaughton, Enid's son. Note the preponderance of girls!

monument to the solid industrial families, like the Kitsons, who made Leeds
famous. Aunt Nellie puts a programme
into my hand and we climb the stairs to
our seats. The usherette opens a small
door and we are in a box, just above the
stage. Above our heads, cherubs swoop
on gilded wings. Below, the heavy red
velvet curtains are closed. Suddenly, a
thick white safety curtain descends,
telling us that we shall all be safe if
there is a fire. Once we have absorbed
this information, it rises. In the pit, the
conductor raises his baton and the au-
dience stands for 'God Save the King'.
Soon, the curtains draw back to reveal
a night nursery containing the Darling

Jill aged five in the stable yard at Longwood, our home on the edge of Leeds, 1930.

children, Peter and Wendy. Nana, a large sheepdog, ambles across
the stage. In a moment, Peter leaps upon the bed and flies out of
the window to the Never-Never Land. Later I cower in my seat as
the crocodile, with a large alarm clock ticking inside him, heralds
the arrival of Captain Hook This sinister figure struts about the
stage waving his hooked arm. Tinker Bell, the fairy, her light now
growing dim and darting in panic from side to side of the wide
auditorium, is about to die, but a loud shout of 'YES' in answer to
the question 'Do you believe in fairies?' restores her to life. The
magic of *Peter Pan* never fails.

For the moment, we led an untroubled life. Each morning, my
father left for 'The Works' in his Alvis. 'What does Daddy do every
day?' I asked my mother. 'He goes to make our bread and butter.' I
was puzzled. 'How does Daddy put the crust on?'

But the bread and butter will soon run out. During the General
Strike, four years earlier, my father, with others, drove a train.
Now it is 1930, and economic depression has crossed the Atlantic;
factories around the country are laying off workers. Since his marriage, my father has had a rich benefactor who has given his

Peggy and Jill
aged three and
five, *c* 1929.
Peggy has had her
hair brushed into
what she called
'My Thames
Tunnel'.

unskilled son-in-law a job, of sorts.[9] Each day he drives off to
Monkbridge, the Kitson family's iron and steel works, and each
evening he returns to a marriage that is already dead.

My mother tells me we are moving. There is no job for Jack at
Monkbridge and his father-in-law can no longer work miracles. He
must try his luck in London. Ena, our Nanny, stays behind, but
May and Lucy, the cook and parlourmaid, come with us as we set
off to the capital.

We did not know it, but our early childhood was over.

Notes
[1] Death certificate 7 September 1920. Alexander George (Aleck) born 10 June
1920.
[2] Death certificate 20 March 1922. Anthony Euan (Tony) born 10 February
1922. He also suffered from eclampsia (fits).
[3] Aunt Kate's face towels, flannel silver bags and blankets, all hand-embroidered
with her initials 'KG', may be found in my linen cupboard.
[4] Always pronounced by my father as 'forrid', the spelling of which puzzled me
for years.

⁵ The two elder sons of Geoffrey Kitson. Their younger brother, Timothy, was Conservative MP for Richmond, North Yorkshire, from 1959 to 1983 and served as Parliamentary Private Secretary to Edward Heath when he was Prime Minister. Timothy was knighted in 1974.

⁶ Helen, the daughter of Euphans, my grandfather McNaughton's only sister.

⁷ His father, Sir Charles Barry, was the architect of the Palace of Westminster.

⁸ Ellen, the eldest child of Frederick William, the eldest son of James Kitson I (1858–1948).

⁹ I have no idea what he did.

Family gathering at number 3, Cadogan Square, in December 1928 to mark Evelyn Nevett's first visit home from Australia, where she had emigrated in 1919. In the back row are Sylvia Connor, Noel Harris, Jack McNaughton with Jill, Will Shiell, Stewart McNaughton and Halstead Connor. Seated are Thelma Harris with Beryl; Angela Goff with Stephen; Evelyn Nevett with Anne; Grandfather Airedale; Granny Airedale; Doris McNaughton with Peggy; Violet Shiell with Cynthia; and Enid McNaughton with Margaret. In the front row are Joyce Harris, Jane Nevett, John Shiell and Ronald McNaughton.

Box Hill, Surrey, at the Whitsun Bank Holiday, 1931 – the England I remember from my childhood.

Chapter 2

Uprooted

'For do we must what force will have us do.
Set on towards London.'

Richard II 3.3.208–09

It is 5 January 1931. I am sure of the date for henceforward all my
milestones are royal. This morning my mother picks up the *Daily
Telegraph* and tells us that The Princess Royal has died. Louise
Victoria Alexandra Dagmar, the daughter of King Edward VII and
the sister of King George V, was 63 years old. The date is etched in
memory.

My parents, Peggy and I were sitting at a small gate-legged table
having breakfast in a tiny flat high above Warwick Road, Earl's
Court. A plate of cut brown bread, the butter spread so thinly that
it looked like the ripples on a sandy beach, was before us. It was not
a salubrious area, but it was the best my father could manage while
he searched for a more permanent home. Did he search or did my
mother? Below, the traffic roared up the road on its way to Kensington High Street and Olympia. Peggy and I were slow eaters
and, on the advice of her father-in-law, my mother seized the
chance to educate us. We were only five and three, but already she
had leapt upon *David Copperfield*, one of the set of twenty Dickens
volumes he gave her on her marriage. I imagine she skipped some
bits, for Dickens can be ponderous at times, but she persevered
and our imaginations were fired. I can still remember the frisson of
horror at the entry of the sinister Mr Murdstone and his sister into
the Copperfield home.

My bed, for it was a very small flat, was in the passage between
the bathroom and the kitchen, and it was here that I had my first
out-of-body experience. I was drifting off to sleep when I felt myself

floating upwards and looking down on my own body. It was weird, but I was disembodied.

About three months later, my mother told us that we were moving. Number 2, Cromwell Crescent, SW5, a short distance away, became our permanent home for the next seven years. It is still there and evokes many memories as I pass it today. The Crescent, built in the early years of the century and lying on the northern side of the West Cromwell Road, consisted of a dozen houses facing the redbrick Harrods depository. The front door was reached by steps framed by a self-important pillared portico, above which was a balcony. The house, called a maisonette, was divided into two. We had the three lower floors, including the basement, flanked by a narrow area and the back door, which was the tradesmen's entrance. The brass plate at the top of the area steps said firmly: 'No Hawkers, Tradesmen or Circulars'. Later, I asked my mother, 'What is a hawker?' The upper two floors of the house, reached by stairs leading from the outer hall, were occupied by a maiden lady in her sixties, Miss Adelaide Hine-Heycock.

Beyond, was our own front door. In the hall, I heard the comforting tick of the old grandfather clock, brought with our other furniture from Leeds. To the left was the drawing-room containing grandfather Mc-Naughton's two fine breakfront bookcases. On the oval table in the centre of the room stood a crystal wireless set. My father twiddled with a couple of wires which looked like whiskers. They emitted a crackling sound. On the mantelpiece was an ugly green dappled electric clock, much loved by my father. When its brass hands showed ten to six,

'Candlestick' telephone of the type used at number 2, Cromwell Crescent.

26

we knew that it was bedtime. By the window, on a small table, was an upright, black bakelite telephone. When you wanted to make a call, you detached the long tube hanging from its side and spoke into the round mouthpiece. 'Now', said my mother, 'this is very important. You must learn our number in case, at any time, you are lost. It is Western 2848. Do not forget it, or your address. Tell the nice policeman that you live at number 2, Cromwell Crescent and he will bring you home.'

Behind the drawing-room, facing the triangular garden, was the dining-room. Here were familiar pieces, the table, the oak Jacobean court cupboard and the Queen Anne china cabinet, which lives in my own home today. One of my father's favourite Scottish pictures, *The Falls of Rogie*, by his great-uncle James Ferrier, hung above the sideboard. Our Aberdeen terrier, who took his name from this watercolour, had by now been replaced by another, Angus.

Down four stairs from the hall was a half-landing containing the kitchen and a door leading out to the small garden. The kitchen was tiny – only a table where the maids had their meals, a sink for washing-up and a gas stove. Down a further twelve steps was the basement, a gloomy part of the house in which lay our 'schoolroom' facing the street and, behind it, the maids' bedroom. May and Lucy slept in harsh-looking iron bedsteads. Their view of the outside world was of a brick wall and a barred window. In the scullery next door was an ancient knife machine in which Lucy, the housemaid, cleaned the steel knives. It was here, too, that I kept my tortoise, Friday, bought in a pet shop off Kensington Church Street.

Halfway upstairs was another mezzanine floor containing the bathroom. Here was an old weighing machine, with a flap-down front, and a white metal medicine chest on the wall. Inside was a box containing a long glass tube and a rubber nozzle; this was the enema syringe our mother used, with soapy water, to cure our frequent constipation. From the window I could see our garden and the half dozen or so on each side. Up more stairs were the three bedrooms. There was now no question of my parents sharing a room. Their marriage was long past repair, although they tried to hide it from their children. Peggy and I had no idea of the meaning of the separate rooms. My father had the largest, overlooking the Crescent, my mother and Peggy slept at the back, and I was given the smallest room, outside which was the balcony on top of the pillared portico.

* * *

This is the 1930s and children are treated with condescension, patronage and duplicity. 'Come along, dear,' says the nurse. 'We'll just go upstairs for a wee, and then we'll come back to Mummy.' We do not. I am in a small nursing home in Knaresborough Place, to have my tonsils out. After climbing the narrow staircase, I am led into another room which smells of disinfectant. I am told to undress and to lie down upon a bed. There is no explanation of what is about to happen and why. A horrid man in a green mask bears down upon me. He attempts to place something rubber over my nose and mouth. I struggle and try to push him away. He is stronger than me and very soon I hear the thudding noise of a huge machine in my head and a nasty smell in my nostrils. When I wake, my throat is very sore. 'Why did you leave me, Mummy? Why did that nasty woman not bring me back to you?' It is the first lesson in a hard world. I am just five years old.

This was the age of deference. Children were still expected to obey the Victorian precept of being seen and not heard. Grown-ups, if not family, were addressed as 'Uncle' and 'Aunt', occasionally the inelegant 'Auntie'. Children were patronised and talked down to. The BBC had a wireless programme called *Children's Hour*. It was, of course, presented by one of these mythical 'Uncles'. This one was called Uncle Mac. (His real name was Derek McCulloch.)

Ten to nine by the grandfather clock and time for school. My mother had found a small day school, at number 7 Cheniston Gardens. Each morning she walked us there. Turning left out of the house we reached the traffic lights at Earl's Court Road. Then we continued until we turned left into Marloes Road, and on past the hospital with its big iron gates and into Cheniston Gardens. At number 7 she left us. This small dame school was owned by Rachel Wilson, a kindly woman in her forties. Peggy was put in the nursery class run by the plump and rosy-cheeked Miss Lowe. I entered 'Transition', presided over by the red-haired, long-nosed Miss Barraclough, who had bright orange lips. There were boys as well as girls in the school, and I made friends with John Proctor, who would shortly go on to 'Gibbs', a well-known preparatory school. Later, he would ask me to marry him and I bought myself a diamond engagement ring in Woolworths. The day started with prayers and I learned to love Miss Wilson's favourite hymn 'Jesu Good Above All Other'. In the craft class we made painted patterns with cut potatoes; we also modelled with plasticine, made pots and did basketwork. On the top floor, I began piano lessons with a sharp-nosed woman called Miss Harrison. She had white hair in a bun and I did not take either to her or to the piano. The pieces she taught me, like 'The Jolly Farmer's Jog Trot', were uninspiring.

At four o'clock, my mother came to fetch us and we walked home in the dusk. As it got dark, we could see the lamplighter, with

The wedding of Kathleen Jefferies and Peter Wilson, at St Bartholomew the Great, Smithfield, October 1933. The bride was a friend of my parents. Peggy is the bridesmaid seated on the left, and I am seated on the right.

his ladder, going down Cromwell Road, climbing up towards the high gas lamps with his long-handled light. We had been learning Robert Louis Stevenson's poem from *A Child's Garden of Verses* called 'The Lamplighter':

> For we are very lucky, with a lamp before the door,
> And Leerie stops to light it as he lights so many more;
> And oh! before you hurry by with ladder and with light,
> O Leerie, see a little child and nod to him to-night.

On another evening, we might meet the muffin man ringing his bell. On his head was a fat cushion, and on this, under a tin lid, was perched his store of muffins.

My mother had brought May and Lucy with us from Leeds, and I often wondered what these Yorkshire girls thought of London. May, though untrained, was a good plain cook. My favourite food was egg cutlets followed by chocolate soufflé. One day, Lucy said she would teach me to make toffee. In a huge saucepan, she boils the sugar, butter and water. When it is a bubbling, golden brown, she invites me to stir it. I grasp the large wooden spoon. To help my small fingers, Lucy puts her own hand above mine. I am not strong enough to resist the pressure and feel my hand sinking into the boiling liquid. I scream in pain and she releases me. The large blisters on my four fingers last for several weeks.

My father's preferred reading was the *Daily Mail*. There was a children's section run by a character called Teddy Tail. We joined his club and were issued with badges which we wore with pride. For some reason, members were known as Gugnuncks and had a secret sign. Whenever we met another, we banged one fist on top of the other and cried 'Gug Gug – Nunck Nunck'.

Scents are evocative, and the smell of the privet hedge and plane trees lining Cromwell Road stirred my nostrils. Behind each of the houses in the Crescent lay a small triangular patch. Some were tended but ours had been neglected. A few spindly spikes of pink London Pride grew here and there. However, each 24 May, Queen Victoria's birthday, I picked lilies-of-the valley to place reverently on her portrait in my bedroom. Peggy had always been a tomboy

Peggy and Jill, aged six and seven, bridesmaids to Kathleen Jefferies, October 1933. We are wearing apricot velvet dresses made by our mother.

Kathleen Jefferies' attendants at St Bartholomew's church, October 1933. My father is pushing forward a reluctant page.

and daredevil and now she invented a dangerous game. Each garden was enclosed by an eight-foot-high brick wall. The neglected soil rose to a height where we could clamber up. We walked along the top, looking down into the other gardens. It was great fun. Fortunately our mother did not find out.

By now, I had made friends with Miss Hine-Haycock, who lived in the flat above. Like all old ladies, she wore a long black dress, reaching to her ankles. I thought of her as very old, though she could not have been more than sixty. She had some sort of Court connection and discovered my passion for royalty. She gave me a miniature facsimile copy of *The Life of Queen Victoria* which I treasured and kept all my life; I have now passed it on to my granddaughter Catriona for safe-keeping.

In July 1934 I was eight and a half years old, and it was now that I started to write. Each Saturday my father handed us a sixpenny piece. Although given by him, it undoubtedly came from my mother. Sometimes I spent it on a packet of chocolate cigarettes which I pretended to smoke in a lofty manner. Often I saved each

32

silver coin to buy some-
thing more lasting. Once
it was a glass inkstand for
my schoolroom desk
bought from Strakers, the
stationers on the corner
of Victoria Road and
Kensington High Street.
Another time it was a
Conway Stewart fountain
pen in mottled green and
purple which I found for
six shillings at W H Smith
near Earl's Court Station.
Although I did not know
it, for my father never
talked about his literary

Peggy and Jill,
aged six and eight,
in dresses made by
their mother.

forebears, writing is in my blood. Each afternoon during the holidays, my mother walked us to Kensington Gardens and Sir
Christopher Wren's palace, where Queen Victoria was born. On
the way back, crossing Kensington Church Street near the Gas
Light and Coke Company, we entered Holland Street and passed a
small stationer's. Here, I bought a small purple-backed notebook
which cost me fourpence.[1] That evening, I opened it and wrote a
dedication: 'This book is for my Mother on her fortieth birthday.'
Inside I started a fairy story called *The Witch with a Long Nose* about
a witch whose hobby was catching children. My mother was a good
raconteur and on our interminable long walks stimulated my imagination with tales of witches and hobgoblins. But the stories we
liked best were her own. 'Tell us about when you were a little girl,
Mummy.' And so she told us of her unhappy childhood with Germanic governesses. She was a lively child and was often punished –
perhaps by the sinister sounding Miss Charlotte Rieschle.[2] Her
mother and father were often away.[3]

So far, the idea of death has not touched me. Although my
beloved grandfather had died the previous year, it is the death of a

stranger that I remember. On 29 July 1934, one of the maids waves the *Evening Standard* in my face. 'Marie Dressler dies, aged sixty-five,' shouts the bold, block headline. I had never heard of Marie Dressler, but Lucy tells me that she is a famous American film star. For some reason, this death, of someone I never knew, lodges in my mind and sends a frisson down my spine. I am just eight and a half.

Although Cromwell Crescent overlooked the busy Cromwell Road, we had our own small village shops 200 yards away. At the confluence of the Cromwell and Warwick roads there was everything we needed.[4] At the chemist, whose window boasted two enormous green and purple jars, we bought Radio Malt and Virol to help us through the winter. 'Aha!' says Mr Marshall, the moustachioed owner, 'here come the Radio girls.' Opposite, on the corner, was a small stationer where I could buy a whip for my top for one halfpenny. Next door was Cullen's the grocer and wine merchant – my father was a good customer although his choice was whisky rather than wine.

* * *

It is a summer's day in Tunbridge Wells and we are on a ritual visit to my godmother. Having no car, because we have no money, my father has hired one for the day. Miss Kitson, the Hon. Emily, my mother's aunt, lives in solitary splendour in a vast house, Tower Lodge, in the exclusive purlieu of Sandown Park. For many years the devoted companion of her father, Lord Airedale, she seems to me a very old lady, although she is only sixty-seven. Her once red hair is white. She is very rich and fully conscious of the purpose of our visit. She has many godchildren and little interest in any of them. Perhaps if I had been called 'Emily' instead of the mundane 'Jill' she might have taken more notice. She sits in a large armchair and I approach her warily. She offers a wrinkled cheek and asks my name. 'Speak up, child. I can't hear you – don't mumble.' She proffers a huge ear trumpet into which I am instructed to shout. Like her father, her brother Albert, her sister Hilda and her niece Sylvia, she is very deaf. Formidable, self-centred and spoiled, at the mercy of a large staff of servants who fleece her, she lives a pointless and unfulfilled life. She might have married Herbert Gladstone, the Prime Minister's son, all those years ago, but chose to stay at her father's side. Does she regret that glittering youth when she was the beautiful young hostess at Gledhow Hall, with so many ardent suitors at her feet?[5]

* * *

My parents are giving a dinner party. This is a rare occasion for they have few friends. The guests are probably family. Even when they are on their own, they change for dinner, my mother wearing a long evening dress, my father a dinner jacket. It is what they have always done. I am a curious child and, though I should be in bed and asleep, I creep downstairs and listen outside the dining room door. The big grandfather clock strikes nine. Suddenly, the door opens and my father appears. 'What are you doing out of bed? Come upstairs with me, at once.' Inside my mother's bedroom, he sits on the oak settle and puts me across his knee. The indignity, for an eight-year-old, is worse than a sore backside. My father delivers discipline – my mother, love. I am not fond of him.

* * *

We had now been in London for over three years. On 9 October, Miss Wilson gathered us all in a downstairs classroom. We sat cross-legged on the floor as she told us some shocking news. King Alexander of Yugoslavia has been assassinated in Marseille on a state visit to France. There are sinister echoes of Sarajevo in 1914.

The following month, on 29 November, the King's fourth son, HRH Prince George, married the beautiful Princess Marina of Greece. London was awash with 'Marina Green' and the little pillbox hat she wore was copied by every milliner. The *Illustrated London News* published a double-page spread of de Laszlo's portrait of the royal couple. I removed it and had it framed to hang above my bed. The Princess's sapphire became my favourite stone.

The next year, on 24 May, Princess Ingrid of Sweden, a great-granddaughter of Queen Victoria, married Frederik, Crown Prince

Portrait of Princess
Marina, Duchess of
Kent by Philip de
Laszlo, 1934.

of Denmark. I started a royal scrapbook and photographs of their wedding filled the first pages.

At the end of that summer term, Miss Wilson told us some sad news. The school had been losing pupils and she could no longer carry on. The boys, including John Proctor, my first boyfriend, moved to local prep schools like Gibbs' and Gladstone's.[6] My mother told us that in January Peggy and I would be starting at Colet School for Girls, the preparatory school for St Paul's Girls' School.

* * *

During this time, my mother's parents, Lord and Lady Airedale, had been a source of support to her. Of all seven girls, she was the only one married to an improvident husband. Despite the carnage of the First World War, all had found spouses. As a clergyman, Halstead Connor, who married the eldest, Sylvia, was presumably exempt from military service; Oscar Nevett, Evelyn's husband, a Rhodes Scholar, earned a Military Cross, like my father, whose brother Stewart survived as a stretcher bearer; Will spent two uncomfortable years interned in Germany after a Bavarian walking holiday in 1914; Noel, unfit for service because of early ill health, became a doctor; and George was far away in India. Although some of them were dull, they were at least solvent. Alone of her sisters, my mother was given a lump sum when she married, which produced an income of £600 per annum.[7] On this she educated her two children, employed two maids and ran the house. My father's contribution was minimal. Most of his money went on drink and greyhounds. He must have been a disappointment to his upright father. We had no car and my mother made most of our clothes.

My grandparents, ensconced in their large house in Cadogan Square, were distant but ever-present. They were passive, rather than active figures. They did not come to stay with us, but their home was always open and welcoming. Granny, although kind, was a tall, rather forbidding figure. She could not have been more than sixty, but seemed already old. Her greying hair was brushed back into a wispy bun. Pince-nez sat on the end of her nose. When she bent down, her wrinkled cheek smelt faintly of lavender. 'Hullo, dear. How are you?' This was the sum of her conversation. Her Germanic nature did not allow her to unbend, and she seemed incapable of affection. Her hands were mottled with brown blemishes. She suffered from flatulence – my cousin Beryl and I tried to suppress our giggles as each small explosion was heard. Never having had much contact with her own children, she did not relate to grandchildren. I do not know how she spent her time in London. Did she do charitable work? Was she on numerous committees? I think it unlikely. Perhaps she read, or did embroidery. I do not think she was intellectual.[8]

Few London houses had lifts, but 3 Cadogan Square was an exception. Having greeted our grandmother, Peggy and I dashed to the back quarters where this monster had recently been installed. For several minutes, we made our stately progress up and down the six floors, until we were told to stop. We halted at the fourth floor to visit 'Mary Nanny', my mother's devoted nurse. Now in her sixties and formerly lady's maid to my grandmother, she had been in the family since her youth, and was much loved. Born in the small Yorkshire town of Malton, she soon became a surrogate mother to the seven sisters.

Trapped in his shroud of silence, my grandfather is a lonely figure. We grandchildren are not taught compassion. His skittish attempts at conversation are ridiculed. We giggle silently behind our hands at his pronunciation of 'fillum' because he has never heard the word. From his large library come the notes of a Chopin mazurka. Despite his deafness, he is a remarkable pianist. The faithful Hemsley, his butler, removes the stubs of half-smoked cigarettes before they fall out of the ashtray on to the grand piano. Music is his solace and he is a generous patron to struggling young pianists such as Solomon, who became world-famous. He and my grandmother have little conversation. Although she has taught herself to lip-read and he has an ear trumpet, communication between them is conducted mainly through his butler. One evening, when they are seated at each end of the long mahogany dining-table, he calls Hemsley to him. 'Please tell her Ladyship that we shall be leaving for Australia in the morning.' This must be something of a shock to my grandmother, but, as always, sangfroid prevails. The servants spend the night packing and next morning all is ready for departure to the New World.[9]

Their seaside house near Deal was open house to their children. My mother, Peggy and I travelled down by train, and, passing each station, Dover Priory, Martin Mill, Walmer, our excitement mounted. There was Pickering, her Ladyship's chauffeur on the platform, and there, inside the car, was her Ladyship herself. She sat behind a glass partition and picked up the speaking tube. 'Drive on, Pickering.' 'Do the children like milk or plain?' I had no idea what she was talking about but guessed it was chocolate. We arrived at Fairfield, a four-storied Victorian house in Archery Square. Behind was a large garden in which we played. The sea, with its shingle beach, was only yards away, and in the night I could hear the mournful cry of the foghorn warning ships away from the Goodwin Sands.

My mother is sitting in the garden on a hot summer's day. She wonders why the three gardeners are looking up into the sky. She looks up too. Her younger daughter, aged four, is pirouetting on the parapet outside the attic window. There is a drop of forty feet to the wide stone area surrounding the house, like a moat. Calmly, she goes to the edge of the area and calls quietly: 'Peggy, what are you doing?' 'I'm just having a look round, Mummy.' 'Well, please climb back inside the window.' My mother takes full marks for her coolness.

The house was run by Mutimer and Mrs Mutimer, a slightly sinister couple who had no connection with the London staff. They were later dismissed – for reasons not discussed in front of the children. Food came up to the dining-room from the basement kitchen on a lift, pulled by ropes. We enjoyed sending it up and down. On fine days, Granny ordered the car and took us to tea on the cliff top at St Margaret's Bay. On Sundays we went to hear the Royal Marines band at their barracks in Deal. The drum major, resplendent in leopard skin and twirling his baton, was an impressive figure.

One day there was a pageant in the grounds of Walmer Castle, for this part of Kent was rich in history. First, the Romans landed on the nearby shingle beach. Then came Hengist and Horsa, Ethelred the Unready, and Harold with an arrow in his eye. I was enthralled and my love of history was kindled: richly caparisoned horses, archers in armour, jousting. Sometimes we walked to Deal along the Promenade, where there were stalls. One of my favourites was a machine that threw little balls into the air – if you caught some in your net, you got your money back. On the pier were more machines, including What the Butler Saw, which we were not allowed to look at. Another printed our names on a metal strip.

All too soon, it was time to go home and to our new school.

* * *

Colet School is the preparatory department of St Paul's. Peggy and I leave the house at a quarter to nine and walk the mile or so towards Hammersmith. Up Warwick Gardens, turn left past Olympia and Cadby Hall and then right into Brook Green. Inside the cloakroom we put on a flowered overall. Prayers are held upstairs – Roman Catholics and Jews are excused. The head-mistress, Miss Wigg, presides. She is probably not more than fifty, but her long black dress and white hair scooped up into a bun make her look older. Her deputy, Miss Hardy, is a large, overweight woman with a permanently disgruntled air. Peggy has the misfortune to be put in her class and they do not get on. My form mistress is Miss da Costa whose long plaited hair is wound round her ears like an earphone. On my report, at the end of that term, she writes, 'Jill is a disturbing influence in class.' For once, my father overcomes his inertia and picks up the telephone – 'What do you mean?' Stymied, she replies lamely, 'Oh! I only meant that she is a bit talkative.'

* * *

1934 becomes 1935. On 6 May, King George V and Queen Mary celebrated the silver jubilee of their reign. My grandfather, as a director, had front row seats on the balcony of the Midland Bank facing Piccadilly Circus (later Swan and Edgar, the celebrated department store) to watch the coronation procession. Our excitement was intense. Peggy and I were almost the same age as 'the little Princesses' Elizabeth and Margaret, and our mother dressed us in the same style: primrose yellow coats with velvet collars (from Bourne and Hollingsworth) and straw hats with flowers round the brim. I was almost ten years old, and clothes were becoming important. It was still dark, but I dressed carefully, never having been up so early before. I put on, for the first time, my new silk stockings and green suede shoes. After a swift breakfast, the four of us left the house in a hired car. London was *en fête*. All the window boxes in Knightsbridge and Piccadilly were decorated with red, white and blue flowers, hydrangeas, geraniums and alyssum. Tall banners of silver lined the Mall. At last, as dawn was breaking, we reached Piccadilly Circus through the early morning traffic. The morning was long, for we were on the return route from Westminster Abbey, but, at last, we heard the distant roar of the crowd as the royal carriage approached. There was the old, grey bearded King and the upright Queen in her flowered toque, waving regally from side to side. Next, came the beautiful Marina, Duchess of Kent, elegant despite her pregnancy. (In those reticent days, royal ladies were never 'pregnant'. A discreet paragraph in *The Times* announced that so-and-so would undertake no engagements until further notice. Everyone knew what this meant.) The day ended late, but, despite our tiredness, it was one we would never forget.

* * *

It is August in Suffolk. Peggy and I are staying with our old Nanny, Ena Kett, and her parents. My mother is having all her teeth out in London – the usual dental treatment for problems – and has sent

Jack McNaughton, c 1935, aged forty-three, ostensibly working, a sad and disillusioned man.

us away. Her husband is acting as aide-de-camp to my grandfather on a golfing trip to Scotland. Here, Jack's gifts of charm and good looks are unsurpassed. He knows how to smooth obsequious maîtres and always stays in the best hotels. Last year, it was Gleneagles and the Roxburghe in Edinburgh's Charlotte Square. This year they are at Rusacks, St Andrews. The waiters grovel to His Lordship, and Jack is in his element. He is a great favourite with the deaf old man and eases any small problems that may occur. My mother is wildly jealous. Why is she never taken away? She, who works so hard and pays all the bills, is never offered a holiday. It is unfair. She has to stay behind to have her teeth out.

Nanny and her parents live in a small cottage, Whinden, high on Black Heath in Wenhaston, a small village near the Suffolk coast. Her father, Harry, has just retired as a London postman. In the past, Peggy and I would sometimes visit their Stoke Newington home – 67 Garnham Street – and play on the swings and roundabouts in the nearby park. Nanny's mother, Mrs Kett, greets us in a multicoloured apron. She is small and bustling. The cottage gate is ringed by orange nasturtiums, and on Sunday mornings we hear the bells of Blythburgh, two miles away. Inside, the cottage smells of oil and of rump steak sizzling on the range. Electricity has not yet reached this corner of Suffolk. All water comes from a deep well, covered by a wooden slab. A bucket on a hook is lowered into its green and slimy depths. Mr Kett keeps a tight hold as we peer downwards. On bath night, once a week, he pours water into two large kettles heating on the hob. Peggy and I sit in the tin bath in front of the range, while Nanny sponges us all over. At the bottom of the garden is a small shed. I open the door and am hit by the stench. I lift the wooden plank and a swarm of flies buzz out of the foetid grey-green depths. On a nail by the door, attached by string, are pages of the local newspaper. It is my first glimpse of rural life, and I leave as soon as possible. I try not to go there at night, for it is scary in the darkness and cobwebs brush my face. There are strange rustlings in the undergrowth.... Each evening, Mr Kett empties the bucket on to his tomatoes.

There are few neighbours, and Peggy and I make our own

games in the dells and hummocks of the heath. Adders slither away beneath the gorse bushes. Suddenly, alarmed, we hear the bell of an ambulance making its way up the sandy track. It stops outside the cottage. A stretcher bearing Mr Kett is placed gently inside. They take him to Halesworth hospital. That evening, Nanny tells us he has died of a heart attack. He was sixty-five. It is our first close brush with death and we are deeply moved. The next day, Aunt Sylvia, who lives near Saxmundham, comes to fetch us.

Sylvia, my mother's eldest sister, was a kindly woman whose life was marred by congenital deafness. Like my grandfather, she was considered childish because she could not hear, and to mitigate this she laughed in a high-pitched cackle. Before her marriage, she almost became a nun, changing her name from Marguerite Emily to Sylvia. But her father would not hear of it – he preferred her to be the bride of Halstead Connor, who had just taken Holy Orders, rather than the Bride of Christ. Halstead was not an exciting man. Solemn, as befitted a clergyman, he seldom smiled. Brother to 'Emmy' Wharton, the Kitson sisters' governess, he preached incomprehensible sermons. Sadly they had no children, and so they were a safe haven in an emergency. Their rectory, at Benhall, was a large Georgian house in an equally large garden. Figs and apricots grew in profusion. It must have been difficult for Sylvia, unused to

Benhall Vicarage, Suffolk, home of the Reverend Halstead Connor and his wife Sylvia.

43

Benhall church
near Saxmundham,
Suffolk.

children, to entertain two small girls, but she did her best. The village shop was full of exciting sweets, like gobstoppers, which Peggy and I were not allowed at home. They changed colour in our mouths and we stuck out our multicoloured tongues at each other. One afternoon Aunt Sylvia took us to Ipswich to see our first film. It was *The Petrified Forest* with Leslie Howard and Bette Davis. The story was above our heads but we relished the adult occasion. On Sundays, we drove to Benhall church, some way from the rectory, where Halstead droned on from the pulpit. We had no idea what he was saying. The Holy Ghost was someone we had yet to encounter.

At home, we occasionally went to church with my mother. My father went to the pub, his spiritual life having been blighted by too much Kirk in his youth.

On other Sundays, we visited my father's cousins at 4 Grenville Place. Here he felt at home. His father's brother, Norman, a successful lawyer, had married Christina Leck, always known as 'An Teenie'. The house and its servants would one day inspire his gifted grandson, John Hawkesworth to write the popular television series of the 1970s, *Upstairs, Downstairs*. Norman and An Teenie had four sons, all glamorous and good-looking. Two, Hamish and Norman, were tragically killed within eight weeks of each other in the First

44

World War.[10] Two were left: Harry, who was enormously fat – something to do with his glands – and Forbes, who was a devil with the girls. He and my mother carried on an animated flirtation. It was so marked that one day I said to her, 'Are you and Uncle Forbes in love?' I was told not to be cheeky, but as Forbes and his wife Betty, an actress, were not happy, it was possible. Harry and Forbes both had sons named Ian who were known as 'Harry's Ian' and 'Forbes' Ian'. There was also Harry's Alistair and Forbes' Colin. The Mc-Naughtons were strong on boys. Their sister, Nell, married an up-and-coming soldier, Ledlie Hawkesworth.[11] Their son, John, known in the family as 'Ginger' because he had red hair, was an arrogant sixteen-year-old at Rugby who could not be bothered with two small girls.

* * *

Back home, as I wake, I hear my father retching out his gas-damaged lungs. I go downstairs to breakfast. The silence is broken by sounds of sobbing. My mother, alone in the dining-room, is weeping. She knows that nothing can restore the love she once felt

Captain Norman McNaughton (*above*) and his brother Lieutenant Hamish McNaughton RFA (*left*), both killed in action, 1917.

Evelyn Nevett and her children in their garden at Camperdown, Victoria, Australia, *c* 1936. *From left to right*: Jane, Anne, Chester, Doris, Guy and Evelyn.

for this handsome but dissolute man. She weeps, not for her marriage, but for her lost illusions. What can I do to help her? I am old enough now to know that this is a deeply unhappy house, though I do not yet understand the meaning of separate bedrooms. They bicker constantly and I kick her under the table, silently imploring her to stop. She, who has so often comforted me, now needs comfort herself. My father dons his black bowler hat and departs for 'the office'. I have no idea what he does. We go off to school. Life goes on.

My mother's unhappiness was solaced by regular letters from Australia. Evelyn, her beloved sister and best friend, had now been away for sixteen years. Her loneliness and homesickness in a strange land were healed by frequent contact with her parents and sisters, but the person who meant most to her was Doris. By now, Evelyn had five children: Jane, a talented pianist; Doris, an attractive girl who was my mother's godchild and was named after her; Chester, her elder son, who would become a bush fire expert; Anne, who was a budding horsewoman; and Guy, already a motor car enthusiast. Their smiling faces shone out in many photographs. To relieve her loneliness, Evelyn had found comfort in religion. A deeply spiritual woman, she joined the Moral Rearmament movement, or Oxford Group, founded some years earlier by Dr Frank Buchman, an American preacher who, wanting to bridge the gap between fascism and communism, offered hope of a middle Christian way. Evelyn was powerfully affected by this philosophy, which gave her strength.

* * *

Easter 1935. We are at Simnel Cottage at Aldington in Kent, which my mother has taken for three weeks. With us are Violet (Vi) Oxenford, my mother's close friend, her mother Mrs Preston, whom we call Gran, and Vi's son John, who is my age. My mother had got to know this family through her sister Evelyn, who had been in the Land Army with Violet's elder sister, Maud (who later died from tuberculosis), during the First World War. Eleven years younger than my mother, Vi, who had been my mother's bridesmaid, was small and very pretty, with a lovely smile. Vi too had made a sad marriage, to a handsome rotter, Frank Davis. They divorced and Vi changed her name to Oxenford. It is an idyllic holiday, probably because my father is not with us and we are spared the constant bickering. I have no idea what he is doing. The Tudor cottage, built four hundred years earlier, has sloping floors and beamed ceilings. Outside, is a small stream, which we dam. Primroses appear in the lane. This is spring and I am happy. One day, we bike to Hythe, six miles away. On the way, we pass an accident. A cyclist, badly injured, lies on the ground. A crowd gathers – someone says he has died.

After three weeks, we return to London. I am eagerly looking forward to eating my chocolates and Easter eggs. My father had said that there were too many to take away. I go to the oak court cupboard, in the dining-room, where I left them. It is empty. 'Daddy, where are all my Easter eggs?' 'Oh, you had far too many. I have given them away to a hospital.' I do not believe him and realise, with sadness, that I do not love my father.

Grandchildren in the garden of Dunearn, Sandwich, August 1935.
Standing: Ronald McNaughton, Mary Shiell, Jennifer Goff, Margaret McNaughton, Beryl Harris, Jill McNaughton (in a home-made dress), Joyce Harris and John Shiell. *Front row*: Angus, our Scottish terrier, Peggy McNaughton, Alison McNaughton, Stephen Goff and Cynthia Shiell.

About this time, my grandparents moved from Walmer to a larger house in Sandwich, nearer the two prize-winning golf courses, Prince's and Royal St George's. They were generous to their family and each August we departed for our month-long seaside holiday. Often some of the twenty-five cousins were also staying. Beryl Harris was a special friend and we had many giggles, especially about Guilia Rimbotti, grandfather's oddly named Italian friend. The house, Dunearn, is a grandiose Edwardian pile built in about 1905.[12] We turn into the gravelled drive, edged by the Lodge, the home of the Pickerings. At the front door, we are greeted by a footman in navy and canary yellow livery. Behind him is the ever-smiling, red-faced Hemsley, ready to lead us into Her Ladyship's presence. She rises from her chair in the large hall, a

48

central inner sanctum, and extends a papery cheek. Next door is The drawing-room
the drawing-room, seldom used but full of priceless antiques, nod- at Dunearn, *c* 1935.
ding Chinamen and pictures. Children are not encouraged to
enter. Where is grandfather? In the distance, we hear the notes of a
Chopin polonaise, played on his Bechstein grand. He is alone in his
silent world.

To the left of the hall was the dining-room, with its long
mahogany table large enough to seat the ever-increasing family. Six
of my grandparents' seven daughters lived in England, so with
their husbands and children we were often twenty for meals. At
breakfast, we discovered, under the covers of the silver salvers on
the sideboard, sizzling kidneys, bacon, sausages, fried eggs,
smoked haddock and Mrs Hemsley's unforgettable scrambled egg.
If you were still hungry after eating all this (and some of the sons-
in-law were very greedy), there were silver holders on the table
with four boiled eggs in each.

Queen Astrid of
the Belgians,
1906–35.

It was while sitting at the head of the breakfast table on 29 August that my grandmother picked up *The Times* and told us that Queen Astrid, the beautiful wife of King Leopold of the Belgians, had been killed in a car driven by her husband on the shores of Lake Lucerne. She was twenty-nine years old. The Post office issued stamps to commemorate this lovely creature. Another memory for my royal scrapbook.

As the meal ended, my grandmother would rise from the table. 'And would you like to walk round today, dear?' This was addressed to me. Seldom called by our names, we were usually 'dear'. 'Walking round' was the favourite Kitson female occupation. I found it fairly boring, but enjoyed the drive out to Prince's, past the millionaires' smart houses in Sandwich Bay. The sea air was brisk and invigorating. We strode across the links to find grandfather and his male guests. The wind whistled past our cheeks. Peggy skipped along enjoying the feel of the grass on her bare feet. Suddenly there was a yelp. My sister, so accident-prone, had stepped on a piece of jagged glass left by some careless holiday-maker. Bleeding profusely, she was taken off by one of the nannies to have her foot bound up.

Left alone, I am told to return to the house. It is three miles across the sand dunes back to Dunearn. Sandwich is one of the Cinque Ports and the sea has long receded from the town itself. It is while I am walking back, crossing the dykes with care and looking where I put my feet, for the ground is marshy in places, that I have another of my out-of-body experiences. The whole place is silent, the sky is blue and only the gulls, wheeling overhead, make any sound. There is no one else for miles. Suddenly, without warning, I am outside my body. It is an odd sensation to find myself floating, looking down upon the small figure striding towards the distant town In a moment or two, it is over and I am back inside myself.

A little later, Granny suggested that I should learn to play golf. I was not an athletic child but sessions with Mr Hickman, the Pro, were better than the endless 'walking round'. Although I continued to have lessons, I never became any good.

* * *

My mother sits sewing in the fading December light. On her knee is a piece of blue velvet. Soon, we shall be going to the annual Christmas party in Cadogan Square and she is making a cloak for her elder daughter. I have just turned ten, the magic age at which the grandchildren are allowed to attend. She cannot afford to buy such finery, but is determined not to be the poor relation among her sisters, all of whom have provident husbands. She has taught herself to sew, determined that I should be as well dressed as my cousins.

On Christmas Eve, my mother calls me into her bedroom. Taking a bottle of an odd-smelling purple liquid, she pours it carefully into a glass lamp which sits above a small wick. Lighting the wick with a match, she tells me 'this is methylated spirits – you must be very careful.' She places a

Stephen and Jennifer Goff, Angela's children, aged six and three.

51

The four Shiell children, Christmas 1936. *From left to right*: Mary, Cynthia, Janet and John.

pair of curling tongs above the lamp and in a few moments they are hot. She takes a strand of my straight hair and turns it into ringlets.

That evening, my parents and I stand on the marble steps facing the iron-grilled mahogany front door of Number 3 Cadogan Square. Hemsley shows us into the morning-room while he goes to enquire whether Her Ladyship is ready to receive us. As we cross the large black and white tiled hall, there is a faint whiff of Havana cigar. Looking up, I see the huge tree which reaches upwards to the first floor. We climb the stairs and there is Granny, waiting to be kissed.

At the long dining-room table, twenty-two of us sit down to Christmas dinner. Beside each plate is a present, carefully wrapped in Harrods paper. Each year, grandfather sends his secretary to the local emporium to choose something for his daughters. Last year, she came back with six enormous rings. For some reason, perhaps because they thought the choice vulgar, the daughters' thanks were insufficient.[13] This year, as they unwrap their gifts, their faces fall.

Instead of large, expensive pieces of jewellery, they find boxes of Guerlain talcum powder. They are outraged. At the end of dinner, all the sisters, except one, leave the unwanted objects beside their plates. Only my mother, with her business nose, goes round the table gathering up the offending articles, which she later sells to friends.

* * *

On 16 January 1936, I picked up the newspaper to read that 'His Majesty is suffering from a chill.' I thought it odd that something so trivial should be a matter of national interest, but soon afterwards my unease was justified. Four days later, on the evening of 20 January, my parents and I sat in the drawing-room listening to the wireless. My father adjusted the whiskers to get a decent reception. The mellifluous tones of Stuart Hibberd, the BBC's chief announcer, came over the ether. The news was ominous: 'the King's life is moving peacefully towards its close.' It would be many years before the British public learned that these words composed by the Royal Physician, Lord Dawson of Penn, concealed a darker truth. Left to nature, the seventy-year old King, a heavy smoker who was suffering from bronchitis, would have died the following morning and the death would have been announced in the evening papers. This could not be allowed to happen. Lord Dawson therefore resorted to euthanasia, giving the monarch a lethal dose of morphine and cocaine at a time when he was already comatose and close to death.[14] His nurse, Sister Catherine Black, when asked to give the fatal injection, refused, so the doctor had to do it himself. The King died at 11.55 pm. Afterwards, Dawson rang his wife, instructing her to telephone the editor of *The Times* with the news. In this way, the prestigious newspaper was not denied its scoop.

The following morning, the black-edged *Times* tells me that the King's body will be taken to Westminster Hall, where it will lie in state. Its journey from Sandringham, where he died, is solemnly recorded in later issues: the hearse, a gun carriage, is followed by Jock, His Majesty's white pony, bearing the King's boots reversed in the stirrups. The coffin is carried to the small Norfolk station of

Dersingham, where it is placed on the London train. At level crossings and in open fields, silent people gather, bareheaded, paying their last respects. The King's body is conveyed to Westminster Hall, and placed on a purple catafalque. Large crowds arrive in Westminster, the queue of people snaking through Whitehall for almost a mile. They are here to salute a monarch who, though quiet and unassuming, was nevertheless deeply loved. The night before the funeral, his four sons, one standing at each corner of the coffin, keep their silent vigil.

The lying-in-state was a royal occasion that I could not miss. I remembered the times when I had seen this kind old man, white-bearded, the age of my grandfather. Once, bowing gravely from his carriage at the Silver Jubilee, and once when Peggy and I were standing on the pavement outside our house, from his Daimler as it passed on the way to Olympia. Neither would ever forget the cheery wave he gave to two small girls, all to themselves.

My mother promises, that, if we are good, she will take both Peggy and me to the lying-in-state. I am a great reader and cannot bear to go to bed without a book. On several occasions, when I should have been asleep, my mother finds me reading. 'If it happens again,' she says, 'I will not take you to the lying-in-state.' I should have known that, schooled by her father-in-law, my mother never makes an idle threat. 'Never say something to a child that you do not mean,' was one of his maxims. And so it is, that on the evening of 26 January, my mother finds me reading in bed, by torchlight.

I beg and plead, but she is adamant. My cries that this is a once-in-a-lifetime occasion, which I simply cannot miss, are ignored. She and Peggy leave for Westminster Hall without me. It is a hard lesson but one I never forget.[15]

A few days later, on 29 January, the King's body was taken from Westminster and conveyed to Paddington for its last journey to Windsor. This time my mother relented and took both Peggy and me to Piccadilly where we hoped to glimpse the funeral procession. The crowds were immense. There were no front row seats in a Midland Bank box so we went by tube to Hyde Park Corner and tried to find a vantage-point. There was none. We made our way along Curzon Street and down Half Moon Street but were quickly swallowed up by people. We could hear the roar of the crowds in Piccadilly and the tramp of boots, but could see nothing. Peggy and I were small. The crowd begins to push forward as the procession is heard in the distance. We can see nothing and we feel nothing but the press of people upon us. A tall man offers to hoist Peggy on his shoulders, but we are so tightly packed it is impossible. We are frightened. Sensing danger, we squeeze our way out. It was an unpleasant experience.

* * *

My mother's finances were now so tight that she made a radical decision. A stranger is to enter our household. Miss Kilby, my father's secretary, short and rubicund, her face as nature made it, was coming to live with us. She is to have the large front room, and my father will move into mine. She will spend her evenings and have all her meals with us. I am to sleep downstairs, in the basement, next to the maids. I am not too concerned, for it will be easier to read in bed. My choice of books is eclectic. After H E Marshall's *Our Island Story*, *The Story of Scotland* and *The Story of Greece*, I move on to others. Nearly all are connected with history. One of the first so-called 'grown-up' books is *Dickon*, a sympathetic life of King Richard III by Marjorie Bowen. Margaret Irwin is another favourite author and I devour *Minette*, the sad story of Charles II's sister, married off to the Dauphin at a tender age and banished to France, never to return.[16]

In the schoolroom was a wire-fronted bookcase containing my mother's childhood books. *Black Beauty* was a favourite, and *Froggy's Little Brother*, a Victorian tear-jerker, made us weep. I decided to start a lending library and stuck a membership label inside each book. I called it The Animal Lovers' Library and enrolled my schoolfriends.

While our lives continued in an uneventful way, there was much going on in the outside world. We did not know that George V's prediction about his errant son, 'after I am gone, the boy will ruin

King Edward VIII and
his mistress, Mrs Wallis
Simpson, 1936.

himself in twelve months', was about to come true. America and
Europe were aflame with rumours about the Prince of Wales, now
King Edward VIII, and his passionate affair with Mrs Simpson, a
divorced woman from Baltimore. The British press, thanks to Lord
Beaverbrook, was silent, but the storm was about to break.[17] The
world knew that the King was besotted with this woman and in-
tended to make her his Queen. In October, in an effort to keep it
quiet, Mrs Simpson went to Ipswich where she was granted a
divorce from her second husband, Ernest Simpson. The American
papers screamed 'King's Moll Renoed in Wolsey's Home Town', and
now it was only a matter of time before the British people were
told. On 1 December, the aptly named Bishop Blunt of Bradford
addressed his diocesan conference on the subject of the irreligious
King. Now all hell broke loose. There were frantic meetings between Stanley Baldwin, the Prime Minister, his monarch, who was
holed up at Fort Belvedere, his country retreat, and the hapless
heir, the Duke of York. Queen Mary commented to her weeping

son, 'Here's a pretty kettle of fish.' Mrs Simpson's house was besieged by the press and she escaped to France, vowing that she would give the King up. But Edward was adamant. On the morning of 10 December, he signed the Deed of Abdication and the following night broadcast to the nation. My mother, knowing my royal addiction, allowed me to stay up, and thus it was that I heard Stuart Hibberd once more as the voice of the nation. 'This is Windsor Castle. His Royal Highness Prince Edward.' Into the ether comes the cracked, half-American voice of the erstwhile King. 'I have found it impossible to carry the heavy burden of responsibility and to discharge my duties as king as I would wish to do without the help and support of the woman I love.' A sleek Daimler is waiting at the Castle gate, its engine running. Prince Edward, now the Duke of Windsor, roars off into the night. He had been King of England for less than eleven months.[18]

Meanwhile other events had been taking place. Ten days earlier, on 30 November my mother, Peggy and I got off the number 74 bus in Cromwell Road after a visit to our grandparents. There was a huge red glow in the sky. Later we learned that the Crystal Palace, the big glass edifice built for the Great Exhibition in 1851, had burned down.

My mother's keen sense of history prompted her, one evening, to wake us to watch the slow flight across London of the latest type of airship, the *Zeppelin*. These were still an amazing sight, although the most famous, the *R101*, had gone down in France with the loss of 48 lives in 1930. After the *Hindenburg* crashed in 1937 with 35 dead, these monsters of the air did not long survive.

* * *

My basement bedroom, known as the schoolroom, was next door to the maids and the scullery. At the end of the linoleum-covered passage was the back door, leading to the area. Sometimes an old beggar woman, ignoring the 'No Hawkers' sign at the top of the steps, crept down them and banged on the back door. I pulled the blankets over my head. It was full of my mother's tales of witches and hobgoblins, and I was terrified.

The maids were often out. One day, it is nine o'clock and I am almost asleep. I hear the back stairs creak with the familiar footsteps. My heart begins to beat, for I know what is to come. A face appears above mine, breathing heavily. It smells of whisky. He starts to tickle me. I suppose it is meant to be a game, but I hate it. I want to say 'Stop It' but I can't – he is stronger than me and I am laughing too much. (It is impossible not to laugh when you are being tickled – it is a reflex action.) The tickling continues a long time, for what seems like twenty minutes. At last he gets bored and, with relief, I hear his receding footsteps mounting the stairs. There is nothing overtly sexual, except that he touches my unformed breasts, but today it would be called abuse.

* * *

Although my father and I had nothing in common, he did his best. Unfortunately, we were miles apart. Perhaps he doubted that I was his child, given my mother's chequered youth.[19] His great, and almost his only, love was the books of Rudyard Kipling, to the exclusion of every other writer. I was saturated with tales of Mowgli and the Elephant's Child who was spanked by his uncles and his aunts. Too much Kipling sickened me. (It is not until I married that I learned from my husband, a huge Kipling fan, what a marvellous writer of prose and verse he was.)

My father enjoyed Gilbert and Sullivan, and one evening he took me to hear *Iolanthe* at Sadler's Wells. I was unmoved. Neither of my parents was musical – my mother's taste ran to Ivor Novello and Sigmund Romberg's musical *The Desert Song*. It would be some years before I heard real music.

I feel belittled, unworthy and unloved. His terse comment, years later, when I tell him I am engaged to be married, reveals the gulf between us. All he says is 'Good God!' Only with Peggy, his copper-headed younger daughter, does he relax. They play chess together and read Kipling – something I could never do. This child, conceived so reluctantly, is the joy of his life.

* * *

It is 12 May 1937. The streets of London are ablaze with flags – photographs of Their Majesties King George and Queen Elizabeth, so recently the Duke and Duchess of York – are in every shop window. I have dressed our balcony with the golden Lion of Scotland and the Union Jack. It is today that this shy, diffident monarch, forced to assume a role so roughly thrust upon him, is to be crowned. We rise before dawn and put on our new clothes. After a quick breakfast, we climb into the taxi. Dawn is breaking as we drive along Piccadilly. Once more, thanks to my grandfather and the Midland Bank, we are given front row seats in the branch facing the Ritz Hotel. We have a long time to wait, for we are on the return route from the Abbey, but at last we hear the roar of the crowd. Inside the golden state coach sits the monarch, waving to his people. Beside him is the small woman whose radiant smile belies the steel within.

Thanks to my grandfather McNaughton's influence, my mother was determined that we should see the other side of life. One day, we got on a bus and drove to 'the Slums' in the East End of London. Although it was 1937, there were still airless tenements where whole families lived in one room, without water, electricity or sanitation. The ragged children played hopscotch or football barefoot in the narrow alleys. Dickens lived on.

Sometimes my mother took us to see the waxworks at Madame Tussauds and the Chamber of Horrors with its thumbscrew and rack. A visit to the Tower of London fuelled my love of history. We saw the cell where the little Princes were imprisoned and the block on which Anne Boleyn laid her head. My grandmother had just given me the whole set of Harrison Ainsworth's novels and I was devouring *The Tower of London*. Later, I read *Old St Paul's* and revelled in the gory descriptions of plague and buboes.[20]

Another of our educational visits was to Kew Gardens. In her youth, my mother had been taught to paint and now she bought us nature notebooks – one side plain for watercolours, the other lined for notes. She took us to the Ladbroke Grove baths, where we were taught to swim by the plump and beefy Mrs Schlottman, one of Hitler's refugees. I learned to dive, with a wooden block between my ankles to keep my legs together. I took the lifesaving test and had to rescue Mrs Schlottman from drowning and stop her from pushing me under water. I passed and became entitled to wear the badge of the Royal Life Saving Society on my swimsuit. When we went to the sea, to Birchington or Sandwich, I strutted about with pride, hoping that someone would need to be rescued. I was small for my age and people looked at me with amusement.

We were taught to ride in Richmond Park. My mother had learned as a girl in the Bois de Boulogne where she rode a mare called Gilda. She was an elegant figure in her black side-saddle habit. My usual mount was Spartan, a sweet-tempered gelding, but one day I was put on Cora, whose mood was uncertain. As we trotted in the Park, she saw a horse she disliked from a neighbouring riding-school. In a moment, she galloped after him at full speed. We dashed under trees, my hat fell off and, despite my desperate tugging at the reins, I had no control. First one foot came out of the stirrup, then the other. Exhausted, I hit the ground. I was not hurt, but the experience put me off horses for many years. Peggy, on the other hand, was a keen and fearless rider.

* * *

I am now twelve and it is time to think of a new school. Colet has been a success. I have been learning Latin for two years and have caught the eye of Mrs Hugh-Jones, a gifted English teacher. My mother would like to send me to Switzerland, to Le Chatelard at Les Avants , but she cannot afford it, and in any case it is clear that war is coming. My five cousins, the children of Enid and Thelma, have been sent to Benenden, a new school in Kent. Although they are very happy there, my mother cannot possibly afford it.[21] Mrs Hugh-Jones knows of her straitened circumstances and suggests Cheltenham Ladies' College where her own very clever daughter is a pupil.[22] She thinks I might get a scholarship.

And so it is that, in March 1938, my mother and I find ourselves in Cheltenham. She stays with friends in the town, while I am lodged in one of the College houses, Bayshill Lawn. All the mothers gather with their offspring in Lower Hall, and all boast about their daughters. One has already won an exhibition; another has a scholarship to her present school; a third has been awarded a music prize. My mother cannot think of anything I have done, and feels inadequate. 'I wish you'd put a feather in my cap,' she tells me later.

The examination lasts for three days, with nine subjects. During the Maths paper, the invigilator, a sharp-nosed, red-haired woman, whom I later discover is Mary Coley, the head of Maths, walks round the room while the candidates are writing. Suddenly, she stops at one desk and exclaims, 'You stupid girl'. This should have alerted me to the teaching ethos at Cheltenham. The girl in question, Gwen Heasman, is clever and not put off by this outburst. She wins one of the scholarships. I am unsuccessful but my mother is told I was the next on the list. Small comfort.

In Europe, the situation becomes more menacing every day. Hitler marches into Austria and then threatens Czechoslovakia. In London, gas masks are issued and buildings sandbagged. Chamberlain flies back from Munich waving a piece of paper. 'Peace in our time', he trumpets. It is not to be.

Notes

[1] It lies today in the bottom drawer of the dining-room tallboy.

[2] A member of the Cober Hill household at Cloughton, Scarborough, according to the 1901 census.

[3] My mother's memories of distant and uncaring parents differ from those of her sister Evelyn, who remembered much happiness. Perhaps Evelyn was an easier child than Doris, who once jumped out of a first-floor window after being locked in the room as a punishment.

[4] These small shops were torn down long ago to make the giant junction leading west from Warwick Road towards Hammersmith.

[5] Hilda, red-haired and less pretty, was far more in touch with young people and the world.

[6] Where my future husband shared a desk with Anthony Wedgwood Benn.

[7] My grandfather soon realised his folly when he saw how quickly Jack ran through the money and the remaining six daughters were heavily tied up in trusts.

[8] My cousin, Mary Shiell, was sent to stay with the grandparents for three weeks in September 1939 and found it an unnerving experience. When she

arrived at Beach Court School, Walmer, her friends remarked that she seemed 'very glad to be free of Granny'.

9 This story may be apocryphal but was told to me by my mother.

10 Loretto School Roll of Honour: www.lorettoschool.co.uk

11 Lieutenant General Ledlie Hawkesworth, KBE, CB, DSO (1893–1945); died at Gibraltar on way home from Commanding X Corps in Greece.

12 Now a boys' preparatory school.

13 My mother's was a large, vulgar ruby ring which I sold for £3000 at Christie's after her death in 1976.

14 His action remained a well-kept secret and the truth came to light only in 1986 when his private diary was opened, Dawson having died in 1945.

15 Much later, she told me that she regretted her hasty threat but that, having threatened, she could not withdraw.

16 All are noted in the list in my brown notebook, which I started at this time and is now in my office.

17 Known as 'the Beaver', Lord Beaverbrook, a powerful press baron sympathetic to the King, had been coerced by Winston Churchill to keep the affair out of the newspapers.

18 People wondered what hold this plain, governessy woman had over the King. They whispered that the sexual skills that Mrs Simpson had learned in the shadier quarters of Shanghai anchored him to her. This weak man apparently suffered from premature ejaculation and his mistress knew of Chinese methods to forestall this. It was said that he was a masochist and enjoyed the humiliation of being ordered, in company, to beg like a dog, with a cigarette between his lips, before being offered a light. More details are related in *Spilling the Beans* by Clarissa Dickson Wright, whose mother was close to the Court. (This information may seem extraneous, but it was the crux of the abdication – he could not live without her.)

19 Hence the title of this volume, *Not the Purser's Daughter?* My mother had many boyfriends, one of whom was the purser on the cruise liner in which they travelled to the Canaries, 1925.

20 Sadly, little read today.

21 Cheltenham's fees were £150 per annum as against Benenden's £200 – a vast difference in those days.

22 Siriol Hugh-Jones, later a talented *Vogue* writer who married the broadcaster Derek Hart and died of breast cancer in her forties.

My double cousins, Alison, Ronald and Margaret McNaughton, *c* 1930.

Roycot, the Stansted home of Stewart and Enid McNaughton; the house is nearest the camera.

My mother, Doris McNaughton, still a handsome woman at forty-four.
This studio portrait was taken in 1938 for me to have at boarding school.

Chapter 3

Loss

She was a Phantom of delight
When first she gleamed upon my sight;
A lovely Apparition, sent
To be a moment's ornament.

Poems of the Imagination VIII,
William Wordsworth

I am standing on platform 1 of Paddington Station with my mother. It is three o'clock on the afternoon of Thursday 18 September 1938. Like the hordes of other girls with their parents, I am dressed in a well-cut pale-green flannel coat and skirt, our Sunday rig. They pour on to the train. I kiss my mother good-bye and find a seat in a carriage with three other 'newbugs', as they are known. It is the first day of my life as a boarder at The Cheltenham Ladies' College, and I am miserable.

After Colet School, Cheltenham was a huge change. It is one of the largest girls' school in the country, holding 850 pupils. It was founded in 1854 by Dorothea Beale, a formidable feminist in the stamp of Florence Nightingale who was determined that girls, as well as their brothers, should be educated. It was a laudable aim, and for many years the College led all other girls' schools in academic excellence. In my mother-in-law's time, the early 1900s, it had acquired something of a snob status. In her house, Glenlee, pupils were encouraged to keep a hunter and to ride to hounds. There was nothing of that in my day. Girls came mainly from middle-class industrial or trade backgrounds in the Midlands. The great attraction for most parents was that the school offered first-class academic facilities for comparatively little money (which was why I was sent). One of the girls in my House, Bayshill Lawn, was

Betty Moores, the Littlewoods Pools heiress. Large and with a huge, all-embracing bosom, she can be seen in the house photograph on page 76. She is now Lady Grantchester and the sixth richest person in Britain.[1]

Bayshill Lawn was a large Victorian edifice in Parabola Road. My mother had been asked which House I should enter and, knowing nothing about any of the ten boarding houses, had chosen the one where I had stayed as a scholarship candidate in March. It was a poor choice. She should have known that a House with many vacancies was not good. Everything depends on the Housemistress, and Miss Stenning, a dumpy spinster in her late forties, was a poor specimen. She did not take to me, and the feeling was mutual.

I shared a dormitory with three others: Pat Lawson, a merry extrovert from Nottingham, whom I had met in March; Ann Parry, a shy Welsh child with rabbit teeth; and Claire Reid, an anxious-looking girl from Scotland. Each bed was divided from the others by a curtain. Any girl found in another's cubicle was subject to instant expulsion. As we unpacked, we laid our clothes neatly on the bed, to be checked by Matron. All uniform had to be purchased from the College outfitter, Madame Forma (surely a made-up name) of Dover Street. She was expensive, and sometimes girls from modest homes came with home-made garments. (One such was Faith Eveson, standing behind Miss Stenning's left shoulder in the House photograph – the points of her collar are too long. Most of us were too polite to comment, but the girls themselves were self-conscious.) Among the large amount of clothes we needed were three liberty bodices (devices from which to hang suspenders for our beige woollen stockings – the liberty is presumably from old-fashioned corsets), four knicker linings, three navy woollen bloomers (known as blackouts), and the three mufti dresses into which we changed each evening. My unpacking completed, I put photographs of my mother and Peggy on the bare chest of drawers and longed for home.

Next morning, after a breakfast of porridge, tea and toast, I joined the green-clad river making its way to Prayers. Inside the gaunt mock-Gothic buildings, hundreds of girls, silent girls, converged upon the Marble Corridor, passing the marble bust of the Founder. If a member of staff approached, we flattened ourselves against the wall. At intervals, down the long passage leading to the Princess Hall, were stationed larger girls, like sentinels, who had beribboned medals on their jutting fronts. These were the prefects. There were four grades: Sub, the most junior; the House Prefects, whose ribbon denoted the colours of her House; then the College Prefects, wearing striped green and white ribbons; and finally the six Committee Prefects. All these luminaries wielded enormous power. They could punish any girl caught talking or running in the corridors or cloakrooms. The usual penalty was a psalm to be learned by heart and recited in front of the House Prefects the following day, a terrifying experience (it happened to me).

Prayers began with the arrival of Miss Popham, the Principal, upon the platform. Her small, well-coiffed figure – she had the air and authority of Queen Victoria – sent a frisson of fear through the ranked masses of girls standing to attention before her. The Princess Hall, or 'PH' as it was known, held several hundred pupils. Above us, in the Gallery, which ran along each side of the Hall, sat the distinguished guests, perhaps a visiting lecturer or a prospective parent. Opposite sat the choir. At the back, were the domestic staff, maids, cooks and cleaners, whose presence at Prayers was obligatory.

After an opening prayer from Miss Popham, we sang a hymn – one of my favourites was 'Dear Lord and Father of Mankind'. Then Jacqueline Russell-Vick, a large girl with wild frizzy hair and sporting a dark green ribbon upon her ample bosom, the badge of office as Senior Prefect or Head Girl, strode up to the lectern to read the First Lesson. After a few more prayers exhorting us to good behaviour, Miss Runge, the head of Music, played 'Jerusalem' on the organ, and we filed, silently, to our classrooms.

I was in I.6a, the top set of the year of about sixty girls. (Each year was divided into three sets, a, b and c.) Our form mistress was the masculine Miss Richards, one of the Maths staff. There were about twenty of us in this form, several of whom I had met in March. We sat rigidly to attention at our desks, standing when

Vii McNaughton.

OUTFIT LIST

5 Bayshill Lawn,
Cheltenham.

OPTIONAL ITEMS

These things need not be provided, unless desired; they are in addition to the necessary outfit.

	Home	College	College	House	REMARKS
1 coloured cardigan.			✓		wearing
1 eiderdown or rug.					
1 pair brown Wellingtons.					
*2 pairs navy tricoline knickers.					
*4 vests.					
Stockings for House use only.				✓	
1 pair dancing brown or bronze sandals (if dancing lessons are taken).					
1 or 2 long-sleeved Shetland bodices.					
1 pair warm green knickers (for wear with green silk dress.				✓	
1 green woollen scarf (regulation).				✓	
1 winter frock should be brought in the Summer Term.				✓	
1 extra sheet					
6 hangers					
Séance mural.					

*These are for warm weather only, and are in addition to "chilprufe" knickers and woollen combinations (or "chilprufe" vests) which must be bought in the Summer Term.

Above and below: My school outfit list, carefully ticked off by my mother as we prepared for my first term at Cheltenham Ladies' College, September 1938.

CHECKING COLUMNS | REMARKS

COLLEGE UNIFORM
(from Authorized Firms only)
(Green blazer coat, skirt)

Home	College	College	Home	Item	REMARKS
				1 green waterproof.	
				1 tweed overcoat.	
				1 ~~tweed coat and a skirt~~	
				1 ~~College frock~~	
				5 silk shirts.	
				1 gymnastic frock.	
				1 games tunic.	
				3 flannel games tops.	
				3 cotton games tops.	
				*2 or 3 green cotton frocks.	
				*1 or more shorts dresses.	
				*2 pairs white knickers to wear with shorts dresses.	
				1 green silk dress and knickers to match.	
				*2 pairs green knickers to wear with cotton dresses.	
				*2 or 3 pairs white woollen ankle socks.	
				4 pairs navy "chilprufe" knickers.	
				1 white woollen jersey.	
				1 green felt hat.	
				1 brown felt hat with House colours.	
				College, House and field ties.	
				1 blazer.	
				1 green cardigan.	
				*1 swimming suit.	
				*1 bathing cap.	
				1 pair special gymnasium shoes.	
				*2 pairs regulation fabric gloves (Plant).	

OTHER NECESSARY ITEMS
*These are needed in the Summer Term only.

Home	College	College	Home	Item	REMARKS
				1 pair of brown hockey shoes.	
				1 pair brown lacrosse boots.	
				Lacrosse gloves and brown hockey pads.	
				2 (or 3) pairs brown walking shoes (medium or low heeled).	

CHECKING COLUMNS

Home	College	College	House	Item	REMARKS
				1 pair low, rubber-heeled brown house shoes for College. (Rubber-soled shoes are not allowed.)	Red (Sussex)
				1 pair brown house shoes (medium or low heeled).	
				1 pair brown or bronze evening shoes (medium or low heeled).	
				1 pair brown goloshes.	
				1 pair white games shoes.	
				1 pair bedroom slippers (heel-less).	
				1 green or brown umbrella.	
				2 pairs plain brown gloves (without fur).	
				2 (or 3) afternoon frocks, with sleeves.	
				4 nightdresses with sleeves, or 4 pairs pyjamas.	
				3 (or 4) pairs woollen combinations or long "chilprufe" vests.	
				2 pairs liberty bodices (juniors).	
				2 belts and 2 brassières (seniors). One of these belts should be bone-less, for games. Corselettes are not allowed.	
				4 pairs white knicker linings.	
				6 pairs brown stockings (extra long). Morley's Irmo "Dago," 3/11.	
				4 (or 3) pairs of silk stockings. Morley's "Pepper," 2/11.	
				2 white princess petticoats.	
				24—36 simple white handkerchiefs.	
				1 warm dressing gown.	
				1 warm dressing jacket.	
				1 shoe bag, 2 linen bags, 1 brush and comb bag.	
				1 nightdress case.	
				1 hairbrush and 2 combs.	
				1 clothes brush.	
				1 suit case (or hand-bag) at least 18 in. by 12 in. by 6 in.	
				1 fitted work bag or basket and a supply of Cash's names woven in full	

NOTE.—Articles in addition to the above must not be bought. Trunks should...

Miss Richards read out our names. These recalled the middle-class choices of the nineteen-twenties – Joyce, Sheila, Valerie, Beryl, Monica, Brenda, Shirley, Audrey, Jill.

Although the education at Cheltenham was excellent and I am amazed how much I learned, there was no praise.[2] The staff were imbued with the ethos of denigration, sarcasm and repression that ran through the school like a fault-line. They took their lead from the Principal, whose tiny size belied her dominance. There were no marks or prizes for excellence – no top or bottom of the form – only black marks and Refusals for work badly done. So there was little incentive to excel or to take pleasure in scholarship for its own sake. The academic spark spotted by Mrs Hugh-Jones at Colet School was soon extinguished.

There was no bullying by the pupils – that was done by the staff. Some teachers were verbally sadistic and took pleasure in humiliating their charges. The Maths staff were the worst, probably because they were the cleverest. Thank goodness I was not taught by Miss Blandford – 'Blanny' – a squat, square spinster with the squashed face of a pug dog, who waddled rather than walked. The lash of her tongue terrified timid girls into hypnotised silence. Plain girls suffered – the pretty ones escaped. It was her nature.[3] I knew, of course, nothing about lesbians, but can only imagine, in hindsight, that because they were probably all virgins and possibly homosexual as well, they got some sort of sexual kick from this ritual humiliation. The most normal were the unacademic Gym staff – mostly fresh-faced girls straight out of college. There was Miss Elliott, a jolly Scots lass who rolled her rrrs; Miss Hepburn-Newman, whose upper lip was brown and downy – no one had told her about tweezers; and Miss Cowper, whose name everyone mispronounced (being Cooper, not like the farm animal). But the head of Gym, Miss Townsend, a tall erect woman known as Tigger, had been there too long not to be infected with the habitual use of verbal denigration. One day, as I was leaving the gym, she called me out – 'Jill, get your hair cut – it's far too long – your neck must be absolutely filthy.' This was a typical remark. My one aim, having just arrived, was to leave as soon as possible.

* * *

It is an evening in early December, and there are three more weeks of my first term left. The Housemistress has summoned the entire House of forty girls to the assembly hall as she has something very serious to say. I, being small, am standing in the front row. One of the pianos in the practising wing downstairs has been badly scratched. No girl will leave the room until the culprit has confessed. A horrid thought comes into my head. If I blush scarlet, everyone will think it's me. I feel my face burning with a hot, red flush which spreads to my neck. Miss Stenning's eyes are upon me. Nothing is said. Eventually, after about twenty minutes, as no one has owned up, we are allowed to go.

My first term's report arrives at home at the beginning of the holidays. My father reads it with consternation. The housemistress has only one comment to make: 'Jill must learn that she cannot escape the consequences of wrong-doing by practising deceit.' These remarks are endorsed by Miss Popham, in her 'Principal's Report'. Her only words on the passage of my first term are 'I concur.' My father, for once, is galvanised into action. He picks up the telephone. Instead of demanding an explanation for a statement which amounts to libel, he allows her to prevaricate silkily. 'You must understand, Mr McNaughton, that I have over eight hundred reports to write. I cannot possibly remember each one individually.' Unfortunately, he is a weak man. He should have retorted, 'But if you libel a pupil in such a way, surely you remember?' He should have insisted on an explanation. And, on not getting one, he should have demanded the instant dismissal of the Housemistress. He does not.

On the first day of the spring term at Bayshill Lawn, I am summoned into Miss Stenning's office. 'Oh by the way, Jill,' she says casually, 'we have discovered who was responsible for scratching the piano. One of the maids had a new kitten.' There is no apology for this defamation of my character. Today's parents would sue. It does not endear me to Cheltenham.

* * *

While I was struggling with my first term away, my parents had moved house. There was nothing to keep my father in London – no job, no friends, no marriage. Everyone knew that war was coming, so it was prudent to get away. For some years, they had rented holiday houses in Birchington, a small town on the Thanet coast. Being within easy reach of my grandparents in Sandwich, it was a natural choice.

And so, at the end of that term, it was my father who met me at Paddington. His suggestion that we should go to see *The Mikado* was declined – all I wanted to do was to see my mother and Peggy again. He must have found me an unrewarding child. In any case, I disliked Gilbert and Sullivan.

Many writers produce moving memoirs extolling the virtues of their father and recalling what he has taught them.[4] I cannot do so. I cannot recall a single precept which he gave me, apart from 'don't talk with your mouth full.' This is all the more surprising since he had such an upright father himself. My only memory is of constant denigration. Other people's children were so much better behaved – cleverer – or whatever. Like many handsome men gifted with charm, he was devoid of depth.

The house my parents had rented was called Old Gates and it stood, not far from the cliffs, at the top of a gulley called Coleman's Stairs leading to the beach. It was a pretty house with a charming garden entered by a pair of antique wrought-iron gates. Most people rented rather than bought houses, and I remember my parents debating whether their choice should be Old Gates at £120 per annum or an attractive bungalow called Egerton at £100. I was glad they chose Old Gates. The house, which was built of local stone, was spacious. Most of the rooms were on the ground floor, but Peggy and I had our own two rooms upstairs, a sitting-room and our bedroom, which led out to a balcony overlooking the garden. Due to financial stringencies,[5] there were no resident maids and my mother did most of the cooking. A local girl, Ivy, who had epilepsy, sometimes cooked lunch. One day, we asked her, 'What's

Jill and Peggy at Birchington, Easter 1939, aged thirteen and eleven.

for pudding?' 'Mr Asquith's Pudding', she replied, 'Wait and See', one of his stock phrases. Shortly afterwards, she brought in a suet pudding, decked with currants, called spotted dick. It was bliss, to me, to be out of London, and I was very happy.

Birchington was a small seaside town adjoining Westgate and Margate. Frequent buses travelled between them, but Peggy and I spent most of our time on our bikes, exploring the country. The wind – there was always wind, a bitter north-easterly – stung our cheeks as we rode along the coast road, sheltering when we could behind the big sea wall. We often went off for the whole day on our own, with a picnic lunch. No one worried if we did not come back till dusk. Margate with its garish attractions was a favourite haunt, and the amusement park, Dreamland, our idea of heaven. We whizzed up and down on the scenic railway, or switchback, scared ourselves in the Ghost Train and hooted with laughter as we drove the dodgem cars. There was a good cinema in Margate, the Regal in Cecil Square, and we were now old enough to enjoy films – I was just thirteen and Peggy eleven. A film I remember was *The Tunnel*, a look into the distant future (1940) when a tunnel would be built under the English Channel. There was a dramatic moment when the sea poured in and the chap in charge had to make the hideous decision to close the safety gates, thus drowning his son. A beautiful actress called Helen Vinson took the main part. We also saw *Things to Come*, an adaptation of H G Wells' novel *The Shape of Things To Come*, a war of the worlds twenty or thirty years hence – pretty scary stuff.

All too soon the year was 1939 and I was back in hateful Cheltenham. During the spring term we played lacrosse, which I preferred to the more macho hockey, finding that I was quite a good player. I even won a place in the House Junior Team, which was a surprise.

* * *

Each day began with Prayers in the vast Princess Hall. 'Thou shalt not be afraid for any terror by night,' we sang.[6] But it was terror by day that stalked us. Fear was everywhere. We were forbidden to cough, and almost as soon as Prayers began a dry tickle would start at the back of one's throat. The effort to suppress it, the battle of mind over matter, until one was red-faced and almost choking, was superhuman, but better than the ignominy of walking out before the whole school

Prayers have finished and eight hundred girls prepare to return to their classrooms. The Principal tells us to wait. She is now forty-five years old, and her short white hair is cut in a fashionable bob. Her clothes are expensive. Her chalk-white face is well made up with much blue eye-shadow. She has come from Westonbirt, the smart Cotswold school whose pupils are drawn from the moneyed classes. Miss Popham likes men. When she came for her interview, the female governors voted against her but were over-ruled by the men who succumbed to her flirty eyes and fluttering lids.[7] She is a snob. If she is late for prayers, she will apologise profusely saying she has been detained by Lord Bessborough, the Chairman of the Governors. Her voice is gushing and resembles that of Barbara Cartland, with whom she has much in common.

Now the domestic staff, who always attend Prayers with us, are dismissed. The blinds are drawn and it is clear that something momentous is about to happen. The Principal begins to speak. 'I have a serious and distressing announcement to make. Yesterday, at the concert, one girl, <u>one girl</u> disgraced this illustrious school. I am almost too ashamed to tell you.' (My form, because of lack of space in the Hall, were seated on the stage, and I was in the front row.) She continues, 'There was I, sitting with the Bishop of Gloucester on my right and the Rector of Cheltenham on my left, and I was <u>appalled</u> to see that <u>one girl</u> was sitting so badly that <u>we could see her blackouts</u>.'[8] Her voice rises to a fluting crescendo – 'And the name of that girl is....' Eight hundred girls catch their breath and pray that the name will not be theirs. The chances are 800 to 1, poor betting odds, but to my horror it is the name Jill McNaughton that drops into the void. Every head cranes round to see the miscreant, every girl thanks God that the name is not hers. I cannot describe my humiliation. Oh God, let the floor open and swallow me up. To have to rise, with burning cheeks and march, with my class, out of that hall, conscious that 799 pairs of eyes are following me, is something I shall never forget. What sadistic cruelty and how unnecessary. I vow that I will not remain at Cheltenham a day longer than I must.[9] [10]

This naming and shaming was not an isolated incident. At the end of term, we repeated the charade – servants dismissed, blinds drawn, all the ritual of increasing drama. Again, Miss Popham declared that One Girl had committed the unforgiveable. She continued: 'This morning, a member of staff discovered that the bust of our beloved Founder, Miss Beale, had been desecrated. Upon her head had been placed an upturned DO-MESTIC UTENSIL.' The hush was palpable. We later learned that the culprit, the Head Girl or Senior Prefect, Anne Watt, celebrating her last day in this hated place, had committed this act of defiance. She was apprehended, forbidden to go home and confined to her room for three days on bread and water, or so we were told – the story may have got embellished in the telling.

* * *

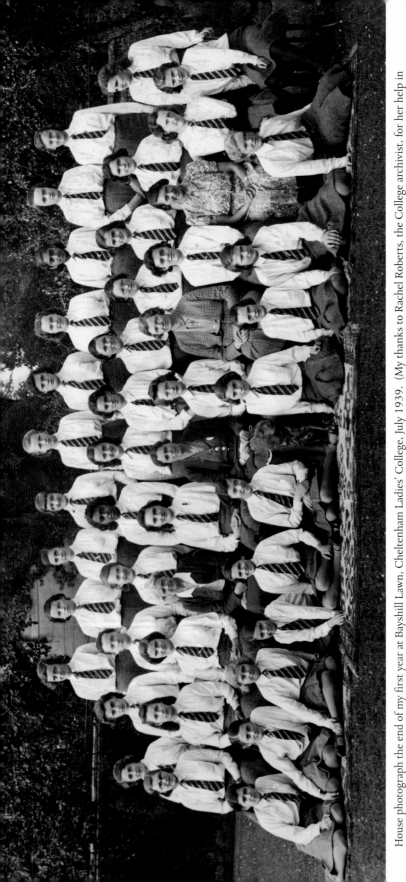

House photograph the end of my first year at Bayshill Lawn, Cheltenham Ladies' College, July 1939. (My thanks to Rachel Roberts, the College archivist, for her help in identifying some names.)

Back row: Margaret Dennis, Catherine Goodwin, Claire Reid, Joan Ford, Brenda Horsfield, Christine Parr, Audrey Walsh, Jaya Jayarainam, Penelope Oscroft, Pamela Brett.

Third row: Monica Foster, Rachel Sutherland, Patricia Borthwick, Josephine Vaughan-Morgan, Jehanaia Jayaratnam, Patricia Burkitt, Faith Eveson, Felicity Abraham, Marjorie McConchie, Marjorie Lewis, Joan Corby, Betty Moores.

Second row: Mona Gosling, Phoebe Cadell, Stephanie King, Miss Darke (Matron), Noreen Ford (Head of House), Miss Stenning (Housemistress), Margaret Crowther, Miss Collier (Second Head), Jonet Roberts, Miss Castleton (Junior Staff), Denise Davidson, Gwen Heaseman.

Front row: Cynthia Crewe, Mary Brander, Faye Levy, Valerie Stockwell, Jill McNaughton, Patricia Lawson, Pamela Stockwell, Ann Parry, Anne Terrell, Alice Robinson.

Peggy and I spent most of the Easter holidays on our bikes, cycling like daredevils along the clifftops where a diabolical north wind off the sea always made progress difficult. Peggy was a happier child now. She had left the hated Miss Hardy behind in London and had become a boarder at Beach Court, a small school for about fifty girls almost on the beach at Walmer. Her cousin, Mary Shiell, was also there and our nearby grandparents were supportive. It was not academic, which was a pity as she was bright, but it was run by a delightful woman, Miss Widlake, who was disabled with a club foot. She recognised her new pupil's potential, and at last Peggy was happy.

The summer term at Cheltenham was more pleasant. The sun shone and I enjoyed learning to play tennis, though I could not see much point in girls playing cricket. I also found that I was quite good at swimming and diving and was chosen to dive for the College Trials. At the end of term, the forty Bayshill Lawn girls and four staff posed in the garden for the House photograph. We were arranged in four ranks – the smallest, of whom I was one, in the front row. Miss Stenning sat in the middle – her petticoat showing.

* * *

We do not know that it is the last summer of our childhood.

On Friday 1 September, Peggy and I sleep out in the garden at Old Gates. It is a brilliant, starlit night, and as I swing in the hammock hanging between the trees I think how lovely it is and how lucky we are to be part of it. In the morning, our parents tell us that Hitler has invaded Poland. The next day, Sunday 3 September, my parents, Peggy and I huddle round the wireless in the sitting-room. Big Ben strikes eleven. The Prime Minister, Neville Chamberlain, is announced. He tells us that he has asked the German Chancellor, Herr Hitler, for an undertaking that his troops will be withdrawn from Poland. His next words are frozen in memory: 'I have to tell you now that no such undertaking has been received and that consequently this country is at war with Germany.'

Almost immediately, as if on cue, the air-raid siren moans.

* * *

Cherry Taggart, a schoolfriend, and Peggy at Birchington gymkhana, August 1939.

We were due back at school within three weeks, but my mother soon learned that the War Office had requisitioned the College buildings at Cheltenham and that the school, or my year of it, was being evacuated to Lilleshall Hall in Shropshire. I was elated. We returned to Cheltenham as usual before meeting the rest of our year and the staff who would go with us. It was all very exciting. We travelled to Wolverhampton by train, with gasmasks in brown cardboard boxes slung over our shoulders. Here we changed for the small market town of Shifnal, from where we were taken by coach to our new quarters.

Built in 1831 by the Marquis of Stafford, later the Duke of Sutherland, Lilleshall Hall was a place of beauty.[11] It was approached through 100 acres of parkland laid out by Capability Brown and along a drive about two miles long. Everything had been organised at short notice and there was a fair amount of chaos. The staff seemed human, at last. Nissen huts, with corrugated iron roofs, had been hastily built in the garden as makeshift classrooms, and the large house adapted to an influx of girls. There were about one hundred of us.[12] I and two others, Dorothy Lennard and Ruth Challis, found our dormitory was in The Top Kitchen. We nicknamed ourselves Doff, Ruff and Jiff.

It is a Sunday afternoon about three weeks after the beginning of term. I am limping painfully up the great staircase. It takes me about a minute to climb one step, for my left knee is a fiery crimson and swollen to the size of a grapefruit. It is agonising to move.

78

The housemistress, Miss Spence, from Roderick, deservedly the 'best' House, who is in charge at Lilleshall, asks me what the matter is. I tell her that I fell in the grounds about ten days ago and that my knee has been painful since then. She asks if I have seen the Matron, Miss Duncombe. I tell her that Matron said she would give me a chit to say that I am excused from games. Miss Spence bends down to examine the knee. She sees that there are two ominous scarlet patches high up on my thigh, almost into the groin. She is horrified and swings into immediate action. I am driven, at once, to the Home Farm, which is the acting sanatorium. A local doctor is called. He says that I must be moved immediately to Newport Cottage Hospital, where an operation will take place that night. There is no time to lose.

Thanks to Miss Spence's prompt action, I did not lose my leg, or die, but it was a close run thing. The idiot elderly matron, who was a St Thomas' Sister[13] and should have known better, had done absolutely nothing except dab it with iodine. I was in hospital for three weeks, and twice a day the two huge gashes in my knee, and the two in my upper thigh, were drained of pus. The four rubber tubes were taken out and fresh ones inserted. It was an agonising procedure without an anaesthetic. There were no antibiotics or penicillin, and I was lucky to survive.[14] Miss Popham, the Principal, came to the Hospital and googooed her pale blue eyes at me, bringing me a box of chocolates. My mother wrote to complain. Miss Popham replied (with a solicitor at her elbow) that 'Although it has the appearance of negligence, my staff are highly qualified and it is unfortunate that Jill is subject to septicaemia.' Again, my parents could have sued

Jill and Peggy in the garden at Old Gates, Birchington, August 1939, with Angus, our Aberdeen terrier.

for negligence. I had missed three weeks of term at lovely Lilleshall, and was very disappointed.

I was even more disappointed to learn, at the end of the Christmas holidays, that Miss Popham had bullied the generals at the War Office to relinquish our buildings and that we were returning, not to Lilleshall, but to Cheltenham. Tiny she may have been, but generals quailed before her.

The winter of 1939/40 was one of the coldest on record. Huge drifts of snow hemmed us in at Old Gates, but we enjoyed ourselves. Peggy was very happy at Beach Court and Cheltenham was not quite so bad now that it was wartime and the atmosphere had relaxed. I did not return to Bayshill Lawn but to St Austen's, a modern, purpose-built house adjoining St Helen's at the top of Parabola Road. Much of the College had been evacuated to houses outside the town, but as our year was the only one that had been sent so far afield we were the only year to return to Cheltenham. The year above had gone to Brockhampton Manor, and the year above that to Cowley Manor, both lovely old manor houses deep in the Cotswolds. The junior school was at Hatherley Court. It was all strange and different from usual.

In May, the war starts in earnest. On 4 June, Miss Smith, the kindly, Eton-cropped Housemistress gathers us all in her sitting-room to hear the new Prime Minister, Winston Churchill. His low, growly voice stirs our blood. Hitler has invaded the Low Countries, King Leopold of the Belgians has capitulated, and thousands of our soldiers are streaming towards Dunkirk. Most are rescued by the little ships, but many are not. France is overrun. An invasion is expected daily. But, says Churchill, if Hitler and his 'Naazi' hordes attempt to invade this island 'we shall fight on the beaches,... we shall fight in the hills, we shall NEVER surrender.'

As the war in Europe gathered momentum, many parents were tempted to send their children overseas to escape the inevitable bombs. Old Canadian friends of my father, the Morriseys, who lived in Montreal, volunteered to have Peggy and me for the duration. I thought it was a splendid idea and the thought of leaving Cheltenham was most appealing. But Peggy would not budge.

Lilleshall Hall, Shropshire, where the second year at Cheltenham Ladies' College was evacuated in September 1939.

She was happy at Beach Court and my parents would not send us separately. Had we gone, the course of our lives would have changed for ever. Tragically, one of the first troopships carrying children across the Atlantic was torpedoed with all lives lost.

Despite the communications difficulties, my mother had kept in close, if sporadic, touch with her sister Evelyn. But while the war in Europe was raging, she had received tragic news from Australia. Oscar Nevett, Evelyn's husband, a brilliant, cerebral man, had died suddenly on 11 June at the early age of fifty-five. An Australian, he had arrived in England just before the outbreak of the First War and enlisted with the Royal Field Artillery. Here he served with distinction, winning the Military Cross. Recovering from being gassed in France, Evelyn, a VAD,[15] had nursed him back to health. My mother longed to be able to comfort her sister, but it was several years before she could do so.

* * *

And now I come to the most painful part of this story.

Peggy's school, Beach Court, had been evacuated from Walmer to a lovely part of Somerset, Clayhanger Rectory, near Taunton. As Old Gates, on the cliff top at Birchington, was almost directly within range of the German firing-line from France and that part of Kent had been designated a Prohibited Area, my parents had to shut up the house and put all the furniture in store with Pettman's in Margate.[16] My father, now forty-eight, had joined the Local Defence Volunteers (LDV), later renamed the Home Guard (and immortalised on television in *Dad's Army*). He was, of course, too old to rejoin his old regiment, The Black Watch, as men over forty were not being taken into the regular army. Instead, he volunteered to join the Pioneer Corps, a hotchpotch of elderly men, mixed with foreigners, émigrés, displaced persons and people of that ilk (including the writer Arthur Koestler).[17] He found himself at Brockenhurst in the New Forest, in a large hotel called Balmer Lawn.

My mother, now homeless, decided to join Peggy. She looked in the accommodation columns of the *Lady* and found rooms with a kindly woman, Mrs Mary Meaden, at Box Tree Cottage in Halberton, a small village near Tiverton. As she had not arrived by the end of term, I spent the first week or so of the summer holidays with Peggy and the rump of Beach Court, now at Clayhanger.

And so it was that, at the end of July 1940, I found myself in a train travelling down to the west country. I was fourteen-and-a-half and felt quite independent on my own. With my bike I changed at Bristol, then again at Taunton, before boarding a small rural train which meandered along a single line towards Exmoor. At Venn Cross, I got out and saw my sister jumping up and down with delight. What a change the atmosphere of that school was from repressive Cheltenham! Miss Widlake, the headmistress, was small like Miss Popham, but warm and welcoming, and I was made to feel really at home. Attached to the rectory at Clayhanger (where the rector and his wife were still living) was a working farm. Each morning Peggy and I went out to collect the warm brown eggs and gather the clotted cream from wide pans in the dairy, with a thick, golden, gooey crust forming on top.

After a few days, my mother, now settled in Halberton, came to collect us. It was the first week of August 1940, and the sky was full of Spitfires and Hurricanes, Junkers and Messerschmitts, for the Battle of Britain had just begun. There were constant dog-fights and trails of white smoke in the sky as yet another plane went down.

Another family was also staying at Box Tree

Oscar Nevett, Evelyn's husband and my uncle, who died in 1940.

Cottage. These were the Goldthorpes, mother and two sons, Robin, a year or two older than I, who was at Dover College, and Dicky, a couple of years younger.[18] We all had our bikes and spent much of the time cycling about the lanes and exploring the country, which was entirely new. On Sunday the 11th, we biked to Bickleigh, and paddled in the fast-flowing Exe.[19]

On the morning of Wednesday 14 August, Peggy and I went to the dentist in Tiverton, and in the afternoon we joined the boys for a picnic tea and bike-ride in the hilly country east of Tiverton. Peggy, who was wearing a bright blue top and matching shorts, was in high spirits and showing off in front of the boys. 'Look,' she called, as she whizzed off down the steep hill, 'No hands!' My mother and I, with the two boys, followed more slowly.

We reach the bottom of the hill which crosses the road from Uplowman to Tiverton. There is one bus an hour. It is stationary in the middle of the road. People are huddled round a bright blue bundle lying on the ground. I put down my bike by the hedgerow and think: 'I shall remember this moment for the rest of my life.'

We approach the small knot of onlookers. A car stops. 'I am a doctor.' He examines the small figure and sees a trickle of blood oozing from her left ear. 'Keep your pecker up,' he says to my mother as he drives off. An ambulance arrives. They lift my sister gently inside. My mother and I climb in too. We travel the short distance to Tiverton. I think of our planned holiday to Newquay in a fortnight's time. 'Oh, Peggy will be better by then,' I think to myself. One of the ambulance men bends down to her. 'She is still breathing,' he says to my mother, as though to comfort her. For the first time, alarm bells ring. 'Why shouldn't she be breathing?' We arrive at the Cottage Hospital. My mother and I are taken into the waiting-room. We wait for a long time. At last, the door opens, and Sister puts her head round the door. 'Are you the mother?' she asks, before disappearing. Another long wait. She returns and puts her arms gently around us. 'Well, my dears,' she says in a frozen voice, 'I'm afraid she's gone.' GONE? GONE WHERE?, I want to shout. (She told us later that she had meant to tell us the first time she came into the room, but could not bear it. She also said that, if Peggy had survived, she would probably have been brain damaged.)[20]

Now, my father must be told. My mother cannot face it and asks Mrs Meaden, our landlady, if she will ring him in Brockenhurst. She picks up the telephone: 'I have bad news. Your daughter has been killed in a bicycling accident.' 'Which one?' 'The elder.' I can almost hear his sigh of relief. My mother corrects her. 'No, I'm sorry, I've made a mistake – it is the younger, Peggy.' Peggy, his 'phantom of delight', his most precious daughter. I don't think he ever gets over it.

We later learned that the bus driver had only just returned to duty after a nervous breakdown. It was his first trip. My mother and I went to see his wife in Tiverton. The poor man was distraught, but there was nothing he could do. 'She came straight into me,' he said.

Even from a distance of nearly seventy years, these August days have been painful to recall. I miss her terribly. The knowledge that I will never see her again, so bright, so light, like quicksilver, is almost impossible to take in.

We buried her in Halberton churchyard. The whole of Beach Court came to the service, and Miss Widlake was visibly moved.

My father never recovered from her death. Seven years later, I wrote a poem about her which I sent him when I was in Paris. He never replied or made any comment. I think it was just too painful.

My poor mother was distraught. She had lost three children, and now the whole force of her love and possessiveness fastened on to me. Until I married, which she did everything to prevent, I would suffer from smother love. It was a hard legacy.

We tried to carry on, the two of us, but it was not easy. We spent a few days after the funeral in Brockenhurst and then went on to Newquay, as planned. I hoped that she would take me away from Cheltenham and send me to Beach Court.

My childhood was over.

Notes

1 *Sunday Times* 'Rich List'.

2 The only praise I received in four years at Cheltenham was from Miss de Gruchy, the Geography mistress, who, when we were evacuated to Lilleshall, remarked that I had 'nice handwriting'.

3 Information from my old friend, Dorothy Lennard, who suffered.

4 See, for example, Blake Morrison's superb memoir *And When Did You Last See Your Father?*

5 My father, although only forty-seven, had no job. Presumably my mother paid for everything, including school fees, from her marriage allowance.

6 Psalm 91, *Book of Common Prayer*

7 Information from my mother-in-law, whose close friend Mrs Philipson-Stow was one of the governors. She said that Miss Popham was a disaster and should never have been appointed.

8 Voluminous black knickers.

9 A cousin to whom I related this story was appalled and said such a thing would never have happened at Benenden, where the staff were uniformly kind.

10 Dorothy Lennard (Doff), whom I recently re-met, after sixty-four years, told me that when she and Ruff (Ruth Challis) came up to my classroom after prayers, to console me, they found me huddled at my desk, with my face in my hands.

11 Now a National Sports Centre.

12 My identity card number (which I can still remember) was OJRQ/29/67 indicating that I was 67th in the alphabetical list.

13 Both she and Miss Spence, I later learned, were St. Thomas' sisters and 'close friends' (information from Joyce Kemp, April 2006).

14 I still have the four large scars.

15 A nurse in the Voluntary Aid Detachment.

16 Many of the Pettman's labels are still on our furniture.

17 See chapter 4, page 92.

18 Robin and I stayed in touch for many years. When he was in the army (Royal Engineers) in India, he used to send me silk stockings. We met after the war, when he came up to Cambridge.

19 Somewhere there is a photograph of Peggy and me, dipping our toes into the water.

20 Death certificate issued by Tiverton coroner following the inquest on 19 August 1940. 'Cause of death: Fracture of the base of the skull due to being accidentally struck by a Motor Omnibus.'

21 Jaa – pronounced *Zhah* – our pet name for each other (see poem opposite).

To Margaret Evelyn McNaughton
Killed whilst bicycling by a Devon General bus
at Batten's Corner, Halberton, Devon
August 14th 1940

We are now approaching Jaa's country. [21]
Does your gay spirit still wander down that Devon lane
Reliving what once was, and perhaps what might have been
As I've so often done?

Can you remember, Jaa, the carefree happiness of heart we felt,
The laughter with no hint of pain
Which was to fall so soon from the already darkening sky?
A stranger, unannounced as is Death's wont,
Came suddenly within our midst, to terrify,
And we could only guess that you must die.

Can it be seven years since you were torn away?
How vivid still that August day!
But in the years between,
Despite the sorrow and the aching emptiness of heart

(We missed you so – the gap has not been filled.)
We have not forgotten you, my Jaa;
Your clothes have not been laid apart
As plucked petals from a living flower wither and fade.
Nor name unspoken, chilling suddenly on lips
That are afraid to bring yourself to mind.

But we have kept your flame alive within our hearts
Tending it jealously from fiercer winds,
That if, one day, you should by chance return,
You need not fear that anything is changed,
Or your dear self forgotten –
How could that be?

Paddington to Kingsbridge, August 7th 1947

87

Chapter 4

Alone

'Irreparable is the loss, and patience
Says it is past her cure.'

The Tempest 5.1.140

It is October 1940, two months since Peggy died, and I am still raw. I had implored my mother to let me leave hated Cheltenham College and send me to Beach Court, but such is her sorrow that she cannot consider so radical a move. Friends are kind and even the staff are softer, having heard of my loss.

The siren has gone. We go down to the shelter in an orderly file followed by Miss Smith, the Housemistress, and her boxer dog, Ferdle. Enemy aircraft are overhead. We are now well-versed in the different engine noises and can distinguish the loud hum of a Spitfire from the distinctive thrum of the Heinkel or Focke-Wulf. In the low glimmer of the blacked-out lamps, we sit on the wooden bunks, chatting. Suddenly, there is an enormous CRRRUMP and the whole building shudders. We know that the bomb is very close. In the morning light we find that it is my old house, Bayshill Lawn, only two hundred yards away, which has been demolished.

My mother was rootless, homeless and husbandless, and her only focus in life was her one remaining child. She decided to come and live near me. In January, Jack's cousin, Betty, once the wife of Forbes and now married to John Leather, a soldier, invited her to 'share' their cottage, The Old Croft, at Brimpsfield, high in the Cotswolds. It was an invitation she came to regret.

My father was now stationed at Donnington, in Shropshire, not far from Lilleshall, and we planned to spend Christmas with him. He booked us into Shrubbery House, a nondescript boarding house in Wellington, where we drank much brown Windsor soup

My father Jack, a Major in the Pioneer Corps, grief-stricken after Peggy's death. This charcoal drawing was made by a friend.

— it was that sort of place. This was one of the coldest winters on record and my chilblains were torture. In our sparse bedroom, where my mother and I shared a feather mattress, the ice in the ewer was two inches thick. (Washbasins with running water did not exist in a house like this.) In the night I plunged my feet into its icy depths, trying to ease the pain. It did not work.

At the beginning of January, my mother and I travelled by train to Cheltenham.[1] We changed at Birmingham, where there were many signs of bomb damage. The taxi, despite its chains, slipped and slithered on icy Cleeve Hill. The snow was deep. We arrived at The Old Croft to begin, as we thought, our new life. I was to be a day girl and was ecstatic.

Betty Leather, the former wife of the flirtatious Forbes McNaughton, was an attractive woman of forty-six, the same age as my mother. Her actressy manner revealed that she used to belong to the Birmingham Rep.[2] Her third husband, Major John Leather, was a taciturn soldier who worked in the War Office in Cheltenham.[3] He looked rather like Basil Rathbone.[4] He and my mother did not take to each other.

The cottage, tucked into the side of a hill, smelt of wood fires and warmth. It was my first taste of country life. Four days after our arrival, I developed mumps. It was not a good beginning – my jaws were so swollen that I could not get a toothbrush between them.

My three weeks in bed were leavened by Betty's fine collection

Jack, at Donning-ton barracks, Shropshire, 1941, a happier man.

of records. It was the first time I had heard good music, and I revelled in it. She brought me *Pagliacci*, Leoncavallo's haunting opera, and Schubert's *Unfinished Symphony*. She also lent me grown-up books. I was now fifteen and my taste was maturing. Beatrice Kean Seymour's *Maids and Mistresses* had ousted Margaret Irwin, and I found out the other meaning of that word. Howard Spring was another discovery,[5] and I asked my mother the meaning of a word which I pronounced 'wor'.[6]

It was unfortunate that, just as I was recovering, my mother caught mumps from me. For John Leather, it was the last straw. He wanted to ship her off to hospital, but was forestalled. Betty's younger son, Colin, aged seventeen, and John's daughter, Jane, an attractive girl of twenty-one, arrived for the weekend.[7]

Although the lanes were still rutted by deep drifts of snow, I biked in the early morning silence to Birdlip, two miles away, where I caught the bus to College. It was heaven to be a day girl and not to have to stay in that hateful place.

One morning, Betty told us that Hilary Strain, my father's first cousin, had married Harold Wyllie, the celebrated marine artist. They had been 'together' for twelve years as Harold was unwilling to divorce his sick wife. She had now died. Betty suggested, with a dirty laugh, that I wrote to Hilly congratulating her on being, at last, an honest woman. I did not know what she meant.

On 15 February, six weeks after our arrival, John Leather announced that 'as Betty has too much work to do, you must find somewhere else to live.' Why does my mother have this effect on men? They are either wildly in love with her or detest her. It is clear into which category John falls.

The ultimatum comes out of the blue. My poor mother, having survived so much sorrow in the last few months, is now faced with another move. Six days later, John Leather, returning from work, throws the local paper at her. 'There are plenty of b and bs [bed and breakfasts] in Cheltenham. I want you out in two days.' She is stunned.

* * *

My mother moved fast, and the next day we were installed at 5 Bath Road, a nondescript house on the outskirts of the town. The landlady, Miss Doris Hart, was a black-haired Jewish woman who dashed about at high speed. The dining-room contained five tables, most of them occupied by single residents, the detritus of war. There was tiny Mrs Dewing, with whom I played piquet and bezique, and Miss Dowding, an angular, white-haired lady who got out of Riga just before the Russians invaded Latvia. Then there were the Beaumonts – mother and daughter. Olga, a greasy copperhead whose ambition was to be a librarian, was also at Cheltenham; her mother was portly and breathed heavily, carrying a faint whiff of body odour. Lastly, there was the darkly saturnine Arthur Koestler. Although he was only thirty-six, there was already an aura of fame and decadence about him. Imprisoned and nearly executed in the Spanish Civil War, he escaped to Britain and had just published his *magnum opus* – *Darkness at Noon*, a dramatic tale of the Soviet treason trials. As an Hungarian émigré he had been interned on arrival in this country, but now wore the uniform of the Pioneer Corps, like my father. He shared his table and probably his bed with his translator, Daphne Hardy, a tall, serious girl of twenty-four. They kept themselves to themselves and did not talk to the other residents.

My mother and I shared a bedroom overlooking the garden for which she paid £3 a week. I bought a blue wind-up gramophone for £4. Betty's catholic taste had woken a chord in me and I started to collect records seriously. I had no idea where to begin, for my mother strayed no further than light opera. My first choice was Tchaikovsky's 'Waltz of the Flowers', my second, the Prelude from Wagner's *Lohengrin* and my third, Joan Cross singing 'One Fine Day' from Puccini's *La bohème*. On the other side was 'They Call Me Mimi' from the same opera. Each record lasted for about four minutes and so needed constant changing. More advanced machines had a central spindle on which one could hang six discs, but this was a cheap buy. Although I danced round the room to Tchaikovsky's lovely music, neither of us could forget the bright-eyed sister who had left us so suddenly, only six months earlier.

All this time, my mother was suffering, not only from Peggy's death and her husband's indifference, but from her rejection by the Leathers. Together, we tried to fashion a life for ourselves, but it was not easy. I had my work to think about, but she had nothing. Fortunately, she knew a family who lived nearby, the Bests, and spent much time with them. Their daughter, Jessamine, was a redhead who also went to College and there was a son, Robin, who attended the boys' College. Their father was, I think, a policeman. Their house, on the Bath Road, was small and poky, but it was a refuge from the boarding house and its pervading smell of cabbage.

My parents kept up the pretence of togetherness and occasionally Jack came to see us. He had nowhere else to go. Although any feeling I had for him had long since disappeared, I was proud to present this tall, still-handsome man as my father.

At Easter, we all went to St Andrews, for the golf. Despite his poverty, my father's maxim 'nothing but the best' still held and we stayed in the Grand Hotel, a huge redbrick Victorian pile overlooking the Royal and Ancient course. I had lessons with Laurie Auchterlonie, the Pro, and did an airshot on the first tee. I was not a natural athlete and would rather have been reading A J Cronin's marvellous novel *Hatter's Castle*, in which I was immersed.

In the evenings, there was dancing in the Palm Court of the hotel to a small string orchestra which played all the latest tunes – 'Lady Be Good', 'The Lady is a Tramp' and, my mother's favourite, Sigmund Romberg's 'The New Moon'. I love dancing, but there is no one to dance with. Over there, on the other side of the room, are two naval cadets, resplendent in Dartmouth uniform. They are accompanied by their mother, a formidable *grande dame* called Mrs Calvert. My mother, who has plenty of self-confidence, is keen to go over and introduce herself, but my father is horrified. According to his Calvinistic nature, it is simply 'not done'. 'You can't possibly do such a thing. We have not been introduced.' So I have to make do with my parents as dancing partners. It is ignominious.

On our way home, we stayed in Edinburgh. Again, nothing but the best would do for my father and we stayed at The Roxburghe, a well-known hotel in Charlotte Square. I met my godmother, Aunt

Kate, tiny, birdlike, with twinkling eyes and a merry laugh. She is my McNaughton grandmother's sister.

* * *

Back to Cheltenham and the summer term. Although it was nearly a year since my sister was killed, I still missed her deeply. On 16 June, I wrote in my diary: 'In Aural Theory we saw a picture which illustrated Chopin's Funeral March. A soul going to Heaven. Lots of lovely angels. Wondered if it was like that for Jaa [our pet name for each other].' Music was a solace and musical appreciation exhilarating. We listened to 'Mars' from *The Planets*, and I was shocked to learn that my father had never heard of Holst.

It is almost the end of term. As I am leaving the classroom, Miss Bowden, my form mistress, calls me back. She is one of the few humane women on the staff and I respect her. 'Oh, by the way, Jill,' she says, 'do you want to go to University?' At fifteen, I have no idea what this means and imagine that it is merely an extension of school – an experience I wish to terminate as soon as possible. I reply in the negative. 'Are you quite sure? You might change your mind later on.' I confirm that I am 'quite sure'. 'Then there is no point in taking Latin for School Certificate.' This thirty-second exchange, as I am going through the door, will determine the rest of my life.[8] I am quite good at Latin which I have been learning since I was ten, but the lack of it means a bar to Oxford and Cambridge in later life. In an academic school such as Cheltenham, it is incredible that there is no careers advice and that a short conversation can mar one's life. Today's College prospectus talks fondly of 'dedicated staff' and 'pastoral care'. These elements were totally missing in the nineteen-forties. Miss Bowden, who was a kindly woman, tired of the repressive atmosphere and later departed to become head of Francis Holland School in London.

Term ended and the question of holidays loomed. I was an unwilling pawn between parents who actively disliked each other. My mother leant on me because she had no one else, and my father resented the fact that all my love was directed towards her. The summer was difficult. My father had to go somewhere for his leave,

94

so we all went for a week to Barmouth in North Wales. As the train wound its way from Wellington, where he joined us, and meandered through the steep Mawddach valley with the brooding height of Cader Idris above, I was filled with awe. This was unknown country and the mountains, their caps still white, were exhilarating. I was determined to enjoy this holiday. We stayed at the Station Hotel in Barmouth, and, although the sea was sparkling and the hills enticing, the week was ruined by my parents' constant bickering. He could not resist denigrating her, 'What is the right way to drink soup, Jill, to tip the plate away from you or towards you?' Whichever way he had decided was correct, my mother was in the wrong and he enjoyed her humiliation. It gave him a brief sense of power and for a moment assuaged his jealousy and insecurity.

His leave over, my mother and I thankfully bade him farewell and continued our peripatetic life. In Kent we stayed in a boarding-house outside Canterbury, near her friend Violet Oxenford. One day we decided to visit Birchington and boarded the Margate bus. This was still a Restricted Area and security was high. At Sarre, five miles from the coast, the bus halted before a large notice: 'You are now entering a Restricted Zone – all passes to be shown.' Our identity cards were checked by military police. These were essential items and had we lost them we might have been put in a cell for the night until we could prove our bona fides. We got off in Birchington and walked to Old Gates, for such a short time our happy home. The gates were rusty and the garden neglected. Several radiators had burst in the house. The whole place looked forlorn. The owners had long departed to a safer place. Then we went on to Margate to inspect our furniture in Pettman's depository. Miraculously, although so near the French coast, the town had not attracted the attention of the Junkers and Heinkels that were only a short flight away. They were more interested in the dockland areas of Chatham and Portsmouth and left this corner of Kent unscathed.

My grandparents' life had changed radically. Their house in Sandwich was too near the coast and Cadogan Square too vulnerable to bombs. Instead, Stewart, their son-in-law, found them a base in Stansted in Essex. Crown Cottage was hardly a cottage for it housed the two of them and most of their staff – Hemsley and Mrs Hemsley, their butler and cook; Mary, Granny's ladies' maid; Jessie, the housemaid; and others. Stewart and Enid remained solid bastions in a fast-changing world and it was to their house, Roycot, on the A11 to Cambridge, that my mother and I travelled in September.

My parent's marital situation was difficult for them, for Jack was Stewart's brother and Enid my mother's sister. But they remained constant to both and were not partisan. Ronald, their sixteen-year-old son, was a few months older than me. Good-looking and eager to please, he suffered the constant denigration of his father, whose preference for his pretty daughters, Margaret and Alison, was not disguised. Sent away to Scotland at an early age, first to Cargilfield, the Edinburgh prep school attended by both his father and his uncle, and then to Fettes, he was an insecure youth. To mitigate this, he was mollycoddled by his mother. My mother always felt that, if she had had charge of him, she could have turned him into a much more confident young man.

* * *

Soon I returned to school to begin the School Certificate year.[9] In English we were studying *Richard II* with Miss Bowden, whose teaching ignited my latent passion for words. Like most children, my Shakespearean education began with *A Midsummer-Night's Dream*, which I must have read at least four times, followed by *The Tempest*. But it was Miss Bowden who first opened the treasure-chest of Shakespeare's language. It is a magic that will last me for life.

Christmas loomed and once more we were to spend it with my father in Shropshire. But first a school friend, Monica Royds, asked me to stay for a few days near Stafford. Her father, a Prebendary, had a parish at Haughton. She had two brothers, John, who was twenty-three, and Clement, two years younger. Both were in the Royal Air Force.[10] John took us to The Bear in Stafford, where we drank gin-and-lime and felt very grown-up. That evening, he played 'The Lady is a Tramp' on his gramophone. I had no idea what it meant. I was just sixteen.

On Christmas Eve I got the bus to Wellington, where I met my mother. That evening, we joined my father in his mess at Donnington, where a dance was being held. It is midnight. The dance is over and I have changed from my long white dress into a short one to travel home. I am in the back of a six-seater army car. My father sits in front with the driver. My mother and his colonel sit behind them. I am alone on the back seat. Suddenly a hand appears from the back of the seat in front. It rests on my knee, burrows beneath my short skirt and begins to travel upwards. I am appalled but am too naïve to dig my nails in hard, which I should have done. It is, after all, the hand of my father's colonel, to whom, I feel, mistakenly, that I owe some deference. By squeezing on the hand for all I am worth, I manage to prevent it reaching the top of my thigh. I am thankful when at last we reach Shrubbery House, where my mother and I are again staying. The whole episode has lasted about forty minutes.

At Shrubbery House, I tell my mother what has happened in the car. She is horrified. She tells my father who, with his Calvinistic upbringing and hang-ups about sex, is appalled.

On 30 December, my mother and I travelled by train to London, where we stayed in the Queensgate Hotel in order to look at secretarial colleges for the autumn. We seemed to spend our whole life in hotels or boarding houses. What a peripatetic existence with no settled home.

* * *

At Easter 1942, we stayed once more near the Oxenfords in Sturry. Being so near the Kent coast, the area was a target for land mines. The village street had been almost obliterated. I wrote in my diary, 'It is tragic for the poor cottagers.'

John Oxenford, a handsome boy, was nearly seventeen and had just joined the RAF. He looked very smart in his uniform. I was now sixteen and, for the first time, attracted a follower. A louche young man, a friend of John, followed me about like a bloodhound. Whenever he called, I disappeared and asked my mother to say I was out. He was unattractive and I did not welcome his attention.

From Kent, my mother and I travelled to Wonersh, near Guildford, where we stayed in The Sheilings Guesthouse. There were stables attached and I took up riding again. My father joined us for a few days, but it was not a success. After he left for Blundellsands, near Liverpool, where he was now stationed, my mother and I walked in a wood thick with primroses. There she told me that she and my father had decided to separate and that he would not be spending any more leaves with us. I was not surprised. The atmosphere recently had been appalling. 'It is a bit of a shock, but I have been expecting it – he never takes the slightest notice of either of us.' I knew that my mother would be much happier without the burden of an improvident husband – she was an intelligent and independent woman who could manage her own affairs. While Peggy lived, they had stayed together – we were a unit, two and two. Now she had gone and there was nothing to hold them. We were a triangle – one and two. I was very close to my mother, and my father must have felt it. Henceforward, there will be just the two of us. I love my mother very much and vow to do all I can to take my sister's place. I do not foresee what a cross this will become.

At the end of April I returned to Cheltenham for my last term. I took nine subjects for School Certificate: English Language and Literature; three Maths papers, Geometry, Algebra and Arithmetic; History; Geography; French; and Scripture. The exams lasted most of June, after which I was free to leave.

* * *

While I was busy working, my mother had been house-hunting. We had decided that I would take a secretarial course. As I have said, there was no careers advice at Cheltenham, apart from that brief question about university, and most girls went into teaching or nursing or embarked on the inevitable shorthand and typing course. During the holidays, my mother and I looked at three colleges, the Triangle in Tring, Mrs Hoster's, which was still in London, and Queen's, which had moved to Englefield Green, a small village near Windsor. We decided on the last.

My mother's sister, Enid, spotted in *The Times* personal columns, a cottage in Englefield Green for the sum of £5 a week. This was really more than my mother could afford on her small fixed income but she decided to take it.

And so it is, that on 12 July, having finished all my exams, I left hated Cheltenham for ever. Four days earlier, my grandmother had died peacefully in Stansted aged seventy-four. She had not looked well for some time and at Christmas had seemed very thin. Although I was almost grown up, I was not told what was wrong – 'some sort of heart trouble, dear'. Many years later I discovered she had been operated on for 'carcinoma of the left breast' in 1933 and that the cause of death is 'multiple secondary carcinoma, toxaemia and exhaustion'.[11] I was still treated like a child and 'breast cancer' was never mentioned.

I wondered what she had left to the world apart from seven daughters. She had a life of ease and was generous to her many grandchildren. I cannot think her marriage was happy but, like most women of her generation, she made the best of it. More than that, I do not know.

Notes

[1] It is from this date that I started to keep a diary, a habit I continued for thirteen years, so the detail is authentic. All unacknowledged quotes are from it.

[2] A well-known repertory company founded by Sir Barry Jackson in 1913.

[3] She was a war widow when she married Forbes in 1919.

[4] A well-known actor who played the menacing Mr Murdstone in the film of *David Copperfield*.

[5] I still have my book list, dating back to 1936.

[6] Whore.

[7] They later married. I believe that Jane already had a three-year-old son from a previous relationship.

[8] It need not have done. I could easily have crammed for Oxbridge. But no one suggested it. Neither of my parents was academic. It still rankles. Mrs Thatcher did a three-month Latin course from scratch to enter Oxford.

[9] School Certificate, the precursor to O levels and GCSEs. Five credits ensured matriculation for university entrance.

[10] Clement was shot down and killed in 1942.

[11] Death certificate, Saffron Walden, 10 July 1942.

Wartime debutante: Jill at Queen Charlotte's Ball, aged seventeen, March 1943.

Chapter 5

Sanctuary

'And changes fill the cup of alteration With divers liquors!'

Henry IV Part 2 3.1.52

Orchard Cottage stood amid farmland at the end of a long track beside a field. Munching grass nearby were two ponies and, beyond them, stood a small white house, formerly a gardener's cottage. It was idyllic.

I had come from Cheltenham by taxi and could not believe our luck. The cottage was reached by a short drive and was almost hidden in the trees. Few people knew it was there. Clarence Lodge, the house to which Queen's Secretarial College had been evacuated, was just outside our garden gate. The Lodge was a large Regency house set in several acres of garden. Lived in for many years by Mrs Jordan, the actress mistress of the Duke of Clarence (later William IV), and their ten children, it had proved a convenient love nest near to Windsor.

Soon after our arrival, there was a knock on the front door. A tall, handsome woman in yellow Fortnum and Mason shoes asked if she might get water for her pony, Romany, who grazed in the paddock next to the cottage. This was Violet Brooke, who, despite her silver hair, was the same age as my mother. She told us that she had two daughters, Rosemary and Gilly, who were nine and seven.[1] Her husband, Charles, was the district manager of Barclay's Bank in Windsor.

Charles' niece, Stella, who was fifteen, lived with them. Her mother had died some years previously, and, as her father and step-mother lived in India, where he was a tea-planter, she had been virtually adopted by the Brookes. She was small and sprite-like, and the fact that she was the same age as Peggy made her very

Stella Brooke (now The
Lady Porter) in 1944,
aged seventeen.

special. For the next seven years, until her marriage, she was as close as a sister.[2]

Early in September, I heard that I had matriculated[3] with credits in English Language and Literature, History, Geography, Algebra, Geometry, Arithmetic and French and a distinction in Scripture. I still did not realise how my decision to drop Latin would affect me later.

On 7 September, I began a nine-month course in shorthand, typing, journalism, book-keeping and Spanish. The girls at Clarence Lodge came from a very different milieu from my contemporaries at Cheltenham. Most were from the landed aristocracy or large Scottish estates, and four or five were the daughters of Earls. There was Anne Ramsay, a pretty brunette, whose father owned Farleyer in Perthshire; tiny Celia Anson, daughter of Lord

Lichfield, whose porcelain complexion resembled that of a china doll; and Penelope Herbert, daughter of Lord Carnarvon, a well-known wit, whose son, Porchester, would become Racing Manager to The Queen.[4] Here too was Elizabeth Lambart, daughter of Lord Cavan and a close friend of Princess Elizabeth, whose bridesmaid she became; Sarah Dashwood, whose father, Sir Francis, the premier baronet, owned West Wycombe Park where the Hellfire Club, famous for its eighteenth-century orgies, was formed; Sonia Graham, who married the future Lord Melchett; Christian Guthrie of Guthrie Castle, Angus; Pamela Tate of the sugar family; and Betty Gregson-Ellis, whose sister, Hyacinthe (always called 'Pussy') married my cousin John Hawkesworth, a Grenadier.

These then were my classmates, some of whom I later encountered in the Wrens. Most of them spoke in high-pitched clipped voices with a nasal drawl that was easy to imitate. After classes, where they were addressed as 'Miss Guthrie', 'Lady Celia' and so on, they dashed up to London to meet their boyfriends, most of whom were in the Household Cavalry, stationed so conveniently at Windsor. Next morning, they regaled the rest of us with tales of their night-time escapades at the Four Hundred or the Milroy, the two most fashionable nightclubs.

My mother's finances were tight – the rent was more than she could afford – so she needed to let our third bedroom. A friend from Cheltenham, Monica Royds (with whom I had stayed in Staffordshire), had also enrolled at Queen's and joined us. For some weeks all went well, but it was soon clear that she did not fit in. She hated shorthand and typing and had an outsize chip. Mrs Royds, an angular, sharp-tongued Vicar's wife rang to voice her disapproval: 'I do not require a room or meal, but will come down to pack her things and REMOVE them. Please send your account to my husband.' A tiresome woman.

Soon afterwards, a policeman arrived at the door to ask if we would take a billetee for two guineas a week – an ATS officer who was working nearby. This was common practice in wartime: people with spare rooms were approached, and, if the house was very large, evacuees were imposed on them. And so Nancy Knox, a jolly girl of twenty-eight, arrived. She was a maths graduate from Queen's College, Belfast, and became a lifelong friend.

Grandfather was now on his own and at half-term invited my mother and me for a week at the Bedford Hotel, Brighton. Here he took a suite and we had our own sitting-room and private bathroom. We were unused to this sort of luxury and I noted, 'We are treated like royalty here. A terrific lot of m'lording.'

* * *

At the beginning of January 1943, my mother received a letter inviting me to be a Maid of Honour at Queen Charlotte's Ball in March. As there were no Courts in wartime, this charity dance took their place and those invited were treated as debutantes. I was delighted – most of the Clarence Lodge girls were going – but where, oh where were we going to find any men? Most men we knew were fighting abroad, some had been wounded, were there any on leave? My mother had a brainwave and, for some reason, asked Guilia Rimbotti, Grandfather's friend (or mistress?), if she knew any. Amazingly, she produced two, a flight lieutenant and a captain. They were not exciting, but it was a coup, all the same.

Clothes were another problem. Not only did I need many coupons,[5] but would I be able to find a dress? We trawled the shops, but dresses were in short supply – there were about six in each. Most were too expensive – eighteen guineas was beyond my mother's purse. Eventually, at Debenham's,[6] we found one in the children's department – a cream taffeta with flowers stencilled on the shoulder and skirt. It was ten guineas.

On 19 March my mother and I travelled to London, where we met Charles and Violet Brooke, who made up our party of six. We were staying at the Cumberland Hotel, Marble Arch, and Violet had insisted upon a double bed. We were amused, on entering their room, to find they had two single beds pushed together. Each girl was invited to have a complimentary facial from Cyclax, one of the leading perfumiers, in the hope that we would use their products for evermore. It worked with me and I used their Special Lotion, for spots, for years to come.

For once, my size was an advantage, and I found myself in the front row of debs as we processed down the main staircase at Grosvenor House. At the bottom, there was a huge birthday cake, in honour of Queen Charlotte, and, like a row of white swans, we swept into a curtsey. The two men produced by Guilia were pretty dull, but at least they could dance.[7]

The debutantes curtsey to Lady Hamond Graeme, the President of Queen Charlotte's Ball, 19 March 1943.

Although my mother had decided upon a complete break from my father, she found it hard to refuse when he pleaded to come for a week's leave. It must have been sad for him to have nowhere to go. At first he was on his best behaviour, but gradually he slipped into his old ways, visiting the Barley Mow, the pub on the Green, 'four or five times a day – he thinks of nothing else.'[8] When he returned, he was morose and bad-tempered after too much to drink. Sadly my mother realised that all she had become was a landlady.

In July, the secretarial course ended and Mrs Cassels, a local resident who had a large house, gave a dance to celebrate. She invited a number of young Irish Guards officers from Windsor: Stella and I were included. The night was balmy, the garden enticing, the men handsome and amorous. Stella caught the eye of Basil de las Casas, long and languorous; my swain was a golden-haired Adonis called

Maids of Honour (continued)

Miss Pamela Filder
The Hon. Barbara Fisher
Miss Mary Wilson Fitzgerald
Miss Sheila French
Miss Naomi Fullerton
Miss Charlotte Gairdner
Miss Fay Wade Gard'ner
Miss Helen Garton
Miss Emily Gibbs
Miss Ann de Courcy Glover
Miss Stella Conway-Gordon
Miss Patricia Greenwell
Miss Pamela Guinness
Miss Christian Guthrie
Miss Audrey Haag
Miss Juliet Hainault
Miss Diana Hallifax
Miss Mary Hambro
Miss Mary Hamilton
Miss Diana Hanson
Miss Rosemary Hartmann
Miss Margaret Harvey
Miss Alison Hawkins
Miss Adrienne Hawtrey
Miss Celia Hedley
Miss Patricia Henkey
Miss Rosemary Copley Hewitt
Miss Eve Hewson
Miss Sonia Favell Hill
Miss Angela Hinchliffe
Miss Barbara Hoare
Miss Sonia Graham-Hodgson
Miss Rachel Phipps Hornby
Miss Rosemary Houldsworth
Miss Elizabeth Howard
The Hon. Miriam Fitzalan Howard
Miss Juliet Howson
Miss Alexandra Hunter
Miss Presily Inchbold
Miss Monica Chater Jack
Miss Angela Jackson
Miss Dorothy Bruce-Jones
Miss Lavinia Jones
Miss Angela Kelly
Miss Bridget Keppel
Miss Joan Rait-Kerr
Miss Pamela Kettle
Miss Helen Killick
Miss Lenerke Knottenbelt
Miss Heather Laing
Miss Jacqueline Laing
Miss Susan Lambert
Miss Jean Landale
Miss Jennifer Howard-Langton
Miss Felicity Latham

Miss Rachel Lauder
Miss Patricia Lawrence
Miss Mary Leacock
Miss Wanda Livingstone-Leamonth
Miss Heather Legge
Miss Martine Legge
Miss Elizabeth Legh
Miss Rosalind Leney
Miss Sheila Levey
Miss Gillian Lightfoot
Miss Diana Lister
Miss Gillian Looker
Miss Marigold Lowe
Miss Angela Lowndes
Miss Priscilla McCreath
Miss Elizabeth MacEwen
Miss Jean MacKay
Miss Katherine McNaughton
Miss Aileen Mander
Miss Felicite Martin
Miss Ayliffe Martin
Miss Elizabeth Martin
Miss Iris Meares
Miss Mary Middleton
Miss Angela Milburn
Miss Sybil Milburn
Miss Maureen Millar
Miss Mary Mitchell
Miss Jean Monteith
Miss Patricia Northcote
Miss Angela Officer
Miss Audrey Oliver
Miss Margaret Ormrod
Miss Anne Orpen
Miss Elizabeth Orpen
Miss Doreen Overall
Miss Grizelda Packe
Miss Penelope Palmer
Miss Phoebe Wavell-Paxton
Miss Sonia Peake
Miss Althea Murray-Phillipson
Miss Barbara Piercy
Miss Pansy William-Powlett
Miss Elizabeth Prestige
Miss Elizabeth Richmond
Miss Leslie Rooke
Miss Marjorie Ross
Miss Heather Royle
Miss Penelope Royle
Miss Susan Rushbrooke
Miss Ann Russell
Miss June Smith Ryland
The Lady Katharine Sackville
Miss Elizabeth Sanders
Miss Jane Scott

Miss Maureen Sharpe
Miss Henrietta Sharpe
Miss Patricia Shaw
Miss Sybil Sherwood
Miss Elizabeth Sinclair
Miss Mary Skinner
Miss Fiona Smith
Miss Mollie Abel-Smith
Miss Christian Abel Smith
Miss Rosemary McNair-Snadden
Miss Rosemarie Sparrow
Miss Charmian Sparrow
Miss Daphne Speir
Miss Ruth Spencer
Miss Cynthia Springman
Miss Ann Steel
Miss Grizel Stewart
Miss Dorothy Stewart
Miss Bridget Stirling
Miss Angela Stokes
Miss Mary Stourton
The Hon. Patricia Stourton
Miss Prudence Strettell
Miss Elizabeth Studd
Miss Imogen Tallents
Miss Patricia Harvey Thomas
Miss Maureen Thompson
Miss Anne Treherne Thomas
Miss Angela Thorp
Miss Camilla Thorpe
Miss Anne Thwaites
Miss Ann Tiarks
Miss Phillida Toogood
Miss Rozanne Upton
Miss Mary Vestey
Miss Adrien Vlasto
Miss June Wadman
Miss Katharine Harrison Wallace
The Lady Camilla Wallop
Miss Elizabeth Ward
Miss Georgina Webber
Miss Veronica Webster
Miss Pamela Wells
Miss Myra Wernher
Miss Ivy Widdersons
Miss Jane Williams
Miss Mary Wills
Miss Audrey Wills
Miss Jane Wilson
Miss Prudence Stewart-Wilson
Miss Elizabeth Winn
Miss Patricia Wood

THE FAVIL PRESS LTD. (T.U.)

APPEAL FOR SERVICE-MEN'S WIVES MATERNITY CARE

QUEEN CHARLOTTE'S

SIXTEENTH BIRTHDAY BALL

for the Débutantes

❋

Hospital Patrons :

HER MAJESTY THE QUEEN

HER MAJESTY QUEEN MARY

OFFICERS OF 1943

Ball President : LADY HAMOND GRAEME
(Vice-President of Queen Charlotte's Hospital)

Organiser : W. SEYMOUR LESLIE
(Secretary-Superintendent of the Hospital)

Ball Secretary : MRS. D. J. KHAN

❋

FRIDAY, MARCH 19TH 1943

GROSVENOR HOUSE, W.1

APPEAL SOUVENIR 2/6

TIME-TABLE

9 P.M.	DANCING to AMBROSE'S ORCHESTRA
10.15 P.M.	MAIDS summoned to assemble
10.30 P.M.	BIRTHDAY CAKE CEREMONY

The Birthday Cake, illuminated by 199 candles, will be cut by THE BARONESS BEAUMONT, THE LADY ELPHINSTONE and LADY HAMOND-GRAEME

11.45 P.M.	CABARET
	GASTON PALMER
	DAWN and CHRISTINE

❋

CAKE CEREMONY

Maids of Honour
(1943 Debutantes)

Miss Juliet Abbey
Miss Charmian Allsopp
Miss Juliet Allsopp
Miss Anne Alston
The Lady Celia Anson
Miss Bridget Assheton
Miss Lorna Baillie
Miss Patricia Bailey
Miss Jane Clinton-Baker
Miss Jill Balcon
Miss Mary Barrios
Miss Valerie Barwick
Miss Jane Bate
Miss Elizabeth Batten
Miss Elizabeth Bayley
Miss Patricia Beauchamp
Miss Anne Beaumont
Miss Everilde Beaumont
The Hon. Ela Beaumont
Miss Patricia Bell
Miss Cara Bell
Miss Elizabeth Leigh-Bennett
Miss Sarah Benson
Miss Elizabeth Blandy
The Hon. Diana Sclater-Booth
Miss Dawne Bovell
Miss Diana Houston-Boswell

Miss Sheelagh Bourke
Miss Barbara Brewis
Miss Rona Briggs
Miss Jane Ruggles-Brise
Miss Jane Buchanan
The Hon. Sheila Butler
Miss Diana Byrom
Miss Elspeth Campbell
Miss Gillian Campbell
Miss Isla Rivett-Carnac
Miss Elizabeth Carnegy
Miss Dorothy Carrington
Miss Patricia Cavendish
The Hon. Mary Chaloner
Miss Daphne Clark
Miss Jocelyn Gordon-Clark
Miss Elizabeth Clarke
Miss Diana Clayton
Miss Barbara Cobbold
Miss Margaret Coke
Miss Elizabeth Collingwood
Miss Frances Colquhoun
Miss Audrey Connell
The Hon. Phillippa Bewicke-Copley
Miss Janet Marshall-Cornwall
Miss Susan Cox

Miss Diana Crosland
Miss Josephone Gordon-Cumming
Miss Alathea Phillips deLisle
Miss Priscilla Dennis
Miss Mary Dennis
The Hon. Margaret de Grey
Miss Helen de Salis
Miss Violet de Trafford
Miss Susan Diggle
Miss Gillian Dodgson
Miss Jean Dodgson
Miss Dawn Drake
Miss Mary Drax
Miss Susan Dugdale
Miss Barbara Dunn
Miss Josephine Dunne
Miss Ann Eden
Miss Marigold Eden
The Hon. Rosemary Elton
The Hon. Margaret Elphinstone
Miss Mary Emmet
Miss Lavinia Emmett
The Lady Diana Errol
Miss Pamela Exham
Miss Joan Faber

'Crawford' (I never discovered his other name). Nothing more than a few passionate kisses were exchanged, for the moral code was circumspect, but next morning both Stella and I imagined we were in love.

* * *

Now that the course was over and I had obtained speeds in shorthand and typing of 120 and 50 words per minute respectively, what should I do? Most of the Clarence Lodge girls had hush-hush jobs in the War Office or Admiralty, found by some well-placed uncle, but my mother, understandably, was reluctant to send me to London. I put an advertisement in the local paper, the *Egham and Staines Gazette*. It was seen by the Hon. Gerald Montagu, who ran a poultry farm near Egham.[9]

As I was seventeen and a half and eligible to enlist, I would have liked to join one of the services, preferably the Wrens. However, my mother did not want to let me go, and I accepted the job at Black Lake Poultry Farm, where I was paid £2 15 shillings per week.

The Hon. Gerald was a large, portly, highly scented man of sixty-three who wore a fawn smock.[10] He had a short goatee beard, black hairy nostrils and thickened speech. He was a name in the poultry world. I soon learned the differences between White Wyandottes, White Leghorns and Light Sussex. The work was dull. His secretary, Miss Shephard, a sour virgin of fifty, had been with him for twenty-five years. She wore her ginger hair plaited in tight coils round each ear. She did not take to me and sought every opportunity to make life difficult.

Each day, I biked down steep Egham Hill, wearing a cycling cloak when it rained. I whizzed through Egham, across the railway line and past Great Fosters,[11] the historic Tudor house recently acquired by Gerald Montagu's nephew, Lord Swaythling. I had an hour and a quarter for lunch in a small café in Egham High Street. Here, I got an excellent three-course meal and coffee for one and ninepence.[12] On the way back, if it was sunny, I parked my bike in a field and sat down to read. A book which enthralled me was Robert Graves' marvellous story, *Wife to Mr Milton*. If it was raining, I sought

Left: The programme for Queen Charlotte's Ball, 19 March 1943.
The names ticked are those of girls I knew or had met.

shelter in the Egham Institute where I could read society gossip in the latest *Tatler* and *Queen* magazines. Many of the glossy photographs were of Clarence Lodge girls, several of them now married.

At Christmas, my mother and I were invited to see the Princesses – Elizabeth and Margaret – perform their pantomime, *Dick Whittington*, at Windsor Castle. The Governor, Lord Gowrie, was a colleague of my grandfather on the board of the Midland Bank and the invitation had come from him. I requested the afternoon off for this historic occasion. 'Quite impossible,' I was told, 'you cannot be spared.' I guessed this was sheer vindictiveness on the part of Miss Shephard, who was always whispering to her boss in the next room. I considered feigning illness but it was my first job and I was conscientious.

Earlier in the year, we heard that John Shiell, Will and Violet's only son, had died of tuberculosis in a Worthing nursing home at the age of twenty.[13] An unhappy and delicate boy, he had not excelled at Eton and was destined for further ill fortune when he joined the Royal Army Corps as a private in 1941. He found tough army life was too much for him and succumbed to ill health.

* * *

By January, the hens and Miss Shephard were beginning to pall. I was now eighteen, the age at which I could be conscripted.[14] My mother reluctantly agreed to let me go. For six months, all the women's services had been closed, but now recruitment had opened again. There was no doubt in my mind which to choose. The uniform alone decided it. The khaki of the ATS was boring, the Air Force blue of the WAAF was not my colour, and, in any case, besides the delicious little hats, the WRNS had far more cachet.[15]

On 5 January, I was summoned to Guildford for a medical. The interview with the Wren officer went well but when I produced a specimen I was called back by the medical officer. 'What did you have to eat yesterday? Your urine is full of sugar.' I racked my brains and could remember nothing but roast beef and two veg for lunch. 'I'm afraid you'll have to come back in a month's time – you may have diabetes.' On the train going home, I remembered that

Nancy, our ATS lodger, and I had made a large quantity of vanilla fudge. This had obviously stymied my chances. I returned in February and, to my great delight, was accepted. Mr Montagu and Miss Shephard were furious. I heard her on the telephone: 'Miss McNaughton has JUST INFORMED me that she is joining the Wrens.' He did everything to block my departure and told the

John Shiell, only son of Will and Violet, who died in 1943.

Admiralty that I could not possibly be spared. He even put my pay up to £3 10 shillings per week as an inducement.

In March, my grandfather died. We had had a big family lunch at The Trocadero the previous October, for his eightieth birthday, but since then he had been failing. He had had an operation six weeks previously, but again I was not considered old enough to be told the cause. My mother and I travelled to Stansted for the funeral. Five of her sisters were there – also a howling Guilia Rimbotti who had hysterics in the Italian manner. Was she his mistress? I cannot believe that he and my grandmother had a very close marriage, but we shall never know. Hemsley was the perfect host. He asked my mother, 'Would you like to go upstairs to view His Lordship?' She assented. Although I was now eighteen and old enough to serve my country, I was not asked.

I had become clothes-conscious and was wearing a small hat with a veil tipped over my nose. It came from Eve Valère, a Knightsbridge milliner, and I was very pleased with myself. Some of the aunts looked at me askance.

Nancy Knox (*left*) Junior Commander, ATS, and Sylvia Giddings, a war widow, at Orchard Cottage, Englefield Green, 1944.

Despite his wealth, my grandfather died a disappointed man. The anguish he expressed on the birth of his third daughter, my mother, rends the heart: 'Another girl.... I am so sorry it is not a boy – I am sure we shall never have one. Three girls are quite enough.'[16] His prediction was correct, but he did not know that he would have four more. The lack of a male heir must have been even more galling for his father, who had risen so far in the great world. At his death in 1911, he had no male grandson, despite having four sons.

My grandfather had much to contend with: the loss of his mother when he was only ten and then the isolating deafness from which he suffered all his life. Even so, after Rugby, he went on to take his degree at Cambridge; he became a Justice of the Peace, a member of Lloyd's and a director of the Midland Bank. The gift of music was his greatest solace, and he was a generous patron of young musicians.

It was grandfather's half-brother Roland who kept the Kitson flame alive. A handsome, distinguished-looking man, he succeeded to the title as the third Baron Airedale. He was a name in the City – a former High Sheriff, chairman of Ford's and a director of the Bank of England when he was only forty-one. His second wife, Christabel, was a tall, good-looking woman of great charm.

Grandfather's death had changed everything financially and my mother did not know how she would manage. Most of the money went to Roland, along with the title. The rest had to be divided

among seven daughters. My uncle Stewart, a chartered accountant, took charge. My mother decided to take another paying guest,
and heard of a thirty-four-year-old war widow, Sylvia Giddings,
who was taking a course at Clarence Lodge. Her husband, an RAF
officer, had been killed in Burma in 1942, and she had a daughter
of four who lived with relations. She was a delightful woman and
had my bedroom.

Mr Montagu's appeal to the Ministry of Labour against my call-
up delayed everything. He told them that I was 'indispensable and
impossible to replace'. It was not until 3 May that I received my
calling-up papers. I was to report to Mill Hill on the 17 May. I was
overjoyed.

Notes

1   In 1952 I introduced Rosemary to her future husband, Michael May Somerville, whom I had met in Burma.
2   In 1949 she married a Cambridge postgraduate, George Porter. He became
    a distinguished scientist, Lord Porter of Luddenham, OM, FRS, President of
    the Royal Institution and Nobel Prizewinner.
3   Matriculation was the qualification for university entrance. Five credits in
    School Certificate were required. For Oxford and Cambridge one of them
    had to be Latin.
4   Famous for the ditty: 'His salad days are over, his little light is out, what used
    to be his sex-appeal is now his water spout.'
5   Clothes rationing started on 1 June 1941. Each person was allocated sixty
    coupons to last one year. The number of coupons needed depended on the
    size of the garment.
6   Debenham & Freebody, an upmarket shop – not today's Debenhams.
7   The Ball programme appears on page 106.
8   Quotation from my diary.
9   Son of Montagu Samuel, a rich Jewish banker, founder of Samuel Montagu,
    created the first Baron Swaythling in 1907.
10 He was one of the first men to wear after-shave: most unusual.
11 Now a luxury hotel.
12 About 8 p today.
13 From 'Miliary Tuberculosis' – death certificate, 9 August 1943. (Today it
    would probably be called leukaemia.)
14 At seventeen and a half I would have been a volunteer.
15 Auxiliary Territorial Service, Women's Auxiliary Air Force, Women's Royal
    Naval Service.
16 Albert to his sister Emily, 28 July 1894.

Wren watchkeepers aboard HMS *Europa*, Lowestoft, April 1946.

Chapter 6

Afloat

'Go make thyself like a nymph of the sea'

The Tempest 1.2.301

The big redbrick building at the top of Mill Hill, formerly the head-quarters of the Medical Research Council, was now the chief training depot of the Women's Royal Naval Service. Here, I spent two weeks, being transformed from a callow civilian into a fully-fledged Wren. The first event, on arrival, was the 'nit parade'. Although the WRNS was considered to be the elite service, the mix of applicants was great. Many were from middle-class schools such as Cheltenham, a few from rarefied Perthshire acres, but many more were from vast conurbations like Leeds and Liverpool. Here, they might live in a back-to-back, with their weekly bath taken in a tin tub in the kitchen, and an outside privy down the end of the block. They became the cooks and stewards of the service – a vital job. Hence the nit parade.

A nurse arrived to inspect our hair and make sure that we were clean. As we lined up, I caught the eye of a tall fair girl with a lovely smile. This was Jean (Jinny) Wyllie, and we became friends for life.[1] As we were both secretaries, we

Jean Wyllie, a life-long friend, aged eighteen, while a Signals Wren serving in Plymouth.

joined Nelson Division[2] where we met like-minded others. They included June Cloudsley-Smith from Essex (we knew many of the same people near Stansted) and Olah Moore, who lived in Canterbury. The four of us ganged up and were together for the rest of the fortnight.

The system was tough – designed to weed out the wimps. At 05.00 each morning we were woken by a loud hooter, known as a klaxon. I was in a dormitory of thirty and had secured a top bunk. We leapt out of bed, dashed to the ablution block, and mustered at 05.30 for 'teaboat' – a mug of tea and a slice of bread and margarine. Then, until breakfast at 08.00, we performed household tasks. I was sent to scrub the floor of the huge assembly hall on my hands and knees. It was the first time I had done anything of the sort – I was lucky not to be cleaning the ablutions. One day, the bread did not arrive at 05.30 and I felt quite faint scrubbing on an empty stomach. After breakfast, baked beans on toast, to provide protein, we attended 'Divisions', the naval term for prayers, in the Assembly Hall. After this was squad drill, where we tried to march in unison and salute. Then there was an interview with the Divisional Officer of Nelson, Third Officer Rosemary Peploe, a delightful girl of twenty-three who decided our Category. This was a huge chance for women whose previous choices had been limited to the dreary trio, teaching, nursing or office work. Now their horizons were limitless. The navy was far-sighted and women replaced men in all but the heaviest jobs. There were engineers, drivers, despatch riders, electricians, meteorologists, welders, carpenters, torpedo loaders, plotters, aircraft cleaners, armourers, telegraphists and mechanics – the list was almost endless. Most of the girls from the large cities became cooks and stewards. The four of us, Jean, June, Olah and I, did a shorthand and typing test. Three of us passed and became SDO watchkeepers;[3] June failed, but, as she had sailing experience, became Boat's Crew, one of the most popular jobs. There was distinct snobbery among the categories: MT[4] drivers, boat's crew and signals were the tops, cooks and stewards near the bottom.

After this, there were lectures on life in the Royal Navy.

We learned how to distinguish ranks and badges; heard about security in Royal Navy ships and how to avoid 'careless talk'; and began to use terms like 'cabins', 'decks' and 'heads'.[5] There were several talks about sex – very necessary when most girls knew nothing. I was lucky to have a broad-minded mother and was fully primed. There was a 'Welcome' talk from the Church of England naval padre. As I had been baptised according to the rites of the Church of Scotland, I listed myself as 'Presbyterian'; when I found that I was lumped with Baptists and Nonconformists, I changed to 'C of E'. On Sunday I joined the others for 'Holy Communion' but could not participate and wished I had been confirmed at school.

Pilfering was rife, and we learned to look after our possessions; one day I noted that 'my nice pen has been pinched.'[6]

In the afternoon we relaxed by playing tennis and swimming at the Mill Hill public baths. The evenings were usually free – sometimes we ate scrambled eggs (made with powdered eggs, a pretty disgusting yellow powder) and doughnuts in the café run by 'Toc H'[7] or fish and chips in the Mess. At other times there were films in the Assembly Hall, including *George and Margaret*, a comedy starring Marie Lohr and Irene Handl, and *Holiday Inn*, a musical with Bing Crosby and Fred Astaire. Night came swiftly – at 22.10 the klaxon sounded for 'Pipe Down' and another day ended.

By the end of the first week, several had dropped out, unable to take the harsh regime. Having endured the toughness of Cheltenham, I enjoyed every moment. Now, a fresh batch of entries arrived and we felt quite superior to these 'newbugs'.

After ten days we were released from housework. After scrubbing floors, I swept and dusted cabins – I was luckier than those who had to clean the ablution blocks. By the twelfth day, we were ready to shed our civilian selves and queued up at Slops for our uniform.[8] Infinitely superior, we felt, to ATS and WAAFs, we put on our navy-blue serge suits and dinky caps. But the serge stockings were a disappointment – only the officers, with their tricorne hats, had silk, for nylons had not yet been invented. The rest of the day was spent marking, pressing and altering our uniforms before we were inspected and 'approved' to appear in public.

As the next day was Whit Monday, the Admiralty generously gave us a half-holiday, called a 'Make Do and Mend' in the Royal Navy.

The four of us celebrated our first day in uniform by travelling to London, saluting every unsuspecting sub-lieutenant we could find. We decided to have a slap-up dinner at Scotts, a posh restaurant in Piccadilly, but were appalled to learn that we had to pay a 'service charge' of four shillings before we could eat a mouthful. The whole meal cost us each eight shillings ('a terrific amount'), much more than the six we earned a week.

Pay Parade, at the end of the fortnight, was a formal affair. We lined up, wearing our caps, and saluted the officer handing out the small, buff envelopes containing twelve shillings. Then we clicked our heels, saluted again and marched off. For one girl, this was too much. She wore her cap askew in a nonchalant manner. When told to straighten it, she replied in a lordly voice, 'Keep your beastly money,' and prepared to leave. This was too much for the pay officer and she was immediately put on a charge.[9]

On the last day, our parents came to see us pass out. My father did not appear, but my mother and Jean's made friends. We marched past, heads high – we were Wrens. Three of us were SDO watchkeepers: Olah went off to Chatham, Jean to Plymouth, and I was sent to Portsmouth. June, as a Boat's Crew, went to Newton Ferrers near Plymouth.

* * *

It is the first week of June, 1944. Everyone knows the invasion of France is imminent and that Portsmouth is the hub. When and where will it happen? We wait.

I travelled down to Portsmouth with Caroline Scott-Montagu, a pretty, fair girl who lived at Beaulieu, not far away. We arrived at the holding depot, a depressing former school, where once more we scrubbed floors until our drafts came through. The second evening I fire-watched from 23.00 until 02.00. Thankfully, there was no siren – Portsmouth and its prime target, the docks, had been much bombed. Caroline was lucky – her brother was Lord

Montagu, and she was whisked away to work in the commander-in-chief's (C-in-C) office. Snobbery still worked.[10] I, being an ordinary mortal, had longer to wait. I was told to report to the signals officer (SO), in HMS *Marshal Soult*, a First World War monitor now at rest in Portsmouth dockyard.

But first I went to my new quarters, Strathearn Hotel, on the seafront at Southsea. I had, of course, brought my bike, the only possible form of transport. I found that the officer-in-charge, a grey-haired woman called Third Officer Barton, lived in Englefield Green, so this was a good beginning. I shared a cabin with three other girls. That night I wrote to my mother, but could say little as all our letters were censored.

Monday 5 June, 08.00. I bike to the dockyard and find my way through the rutted tramlines, past the caissons[11] where ships are in dry dock, to the iron hulk of the *Marshal Soult*. There is a strong smell of oil and I make my way below decks. At a desk in the signals office sits a short, stout, bespectacled young man in his twenties. Without getting up, he says 'I am Sub-Lieutenant Beswick,' pronouncing the 'w' as he does so. This is the Signals Officer. He looks at me with disdain. He turns out to be a former insurance clerk from Manchester, and the possession of one slim, wavy gold ring on his sleeve has gone to his head.[12] He enjoys throwing his weight around, and I sense that life is going to be difficult.[13]

Marshal Soult was the headquarters of the minesweeping fleet which kept the Channel free of mines. Each day, the Captains of the BYMs and MMSs put their heads through the office hatch to collect their orders.[14] It was my job to receive these signals from the teleprinter, type them out, duplicate them on the Ormig machine[15] and distribute them to the C-in-C's office and the ship. Sometimes I manned the antiquated switchboard with its dozens of brass heads at the ends of long rubber leads like writhing snakes. It was easy to stick one into the wrong hole and cut the caller off, leaving an apoplectic admiral at the other end. There were three Wrens in each watch, and we worked in shifts of 08.00 to 13.00 one day, then the next night from 19.00 to 08.00, and back the following day from 13.00 to 19.00.

Tuesday 6 June. I swing gently in my hammock during the night watch. The evening is quiet with only a few signals and we 'turn in' early at 02.00. We wake to the news that the British and Americans under General Eisenhower have landed in Normandy. It is D-Day. The invasion has begun.

After three days, I was moved to a new watch. Leading Wren Pat Wyatt, who was in charge, was a pleasant red-headed girl who lived in Portsmouth. I noticed that she and the signals officer exchanged glances and touched whenever possible. The atmosphere crackled with sex. I soon learned they were having an affair. Pat was married, and I was shocked. I was also surprised, for the SO was not attractive. He was too short and his plain, pudgy, bespectacled face did not turn me on.

A letter arrived from my father, saying that he will give me an allowance. This was welcome news but, by the same post, my mother told me that he was cutting hers in half and that we would share it. He was meant to give it to her monthly from his army pay, but frequently forgot. She was distraught, for money was tight and she could just manage with her two paying guests. I, at least, got my twelve shillings a fortnight. I told my father that it was out of the question.

It was a week after D-Day. Kay Cathcart, a girl in my cabin, and I volunteered for France. The Wren officer put down our names but said we were unlikely to hear for several weeks until the forward positions were consolidated. In any case, as I was under twenty-one, I needed my mother's permission.

* * *

One day there was a telephone call from a 'Mrs Willy'. This turned out to be Hilary Wyllie, *née* Strain, my father's first cousin,[16] now married to Harold Wyllie. They lived in a small house in Gosport. Harold, a tall, handsome, white-bearded man, had served in all three Services. Now in the Royal Navy, he was commandant of HMS *Foudroyant*, a former French man-of-war transformed into a training vessel for sea cadets. They invited me to lunch. This was my first sight of Hilly, and we clicked immediately, Small, like me, she had the determined McNaughton chin and ready wit. When I bemoaned my size, she said: 'Don't be a goose; why want to be like everyone else when you can be different?' Sound advice. She was a good cook and saved the top-of-the-milk for several days until she could turn it into cream. They had a small boat, *Sapristi*, in which we sailed in the harbour. I loved them both.

Life in Strathearn was fun and the sea air gave me an appetite. I often had two or three helpings of the nourishing food. The main diet was baked beans, but we also had 'Woolton pie' made with vegetables and named after Lord Woolton, the Food Minister who was said to have invented it.[17] Soon I had put on two stone. I began to look like a little fat dwarf. My mother was worried that I had not menstruated since I left home, so I went to see the medical officer. He was a young bachelor and found the problems of Wrens embarrassing. When he learned that I was not married, his mind leapt to one conclusion. I was sent to see the senior medical officer at the barracks. He was more worldly-wise. It was the change of air, food and way of life that had upset my hormones. He gave me some pills and my body returned to normal.

Hitler's latest weapon, the Doodle-Bugs, or flying bombs, were a new threat. They whizzed over Portsmouth at 300 mph, usually landing in open country but sometimes doing enormous damage. They had an unpleasant, sinister whine which disappeared when they were about to land. But, as the war news got better and we captured the French coast, the threat became less – the Allies were thrusting further into France and on 15 August we heard that there had been landings in the Riviera. Then days later came the news that Paris had fallen. It looked as though the war might end sooner than we thought

From time to time, it was possible for me to dash home for the thirty-hour break after ending one watch at 13.00 and returning the next day at 19.00. I left my bike at the station and caught a train to Woking, where I either bussed to Staines or hitched a lift. I had no qualms about hitching – it was the obvious way to get about in uniform, drivers were helpful rather than sinister, and I never had a bad experience.

It was on one of these breaks that Violet Brooke arranged a party. She was a born matchmaker and was determined to find some young men. As we knew from Queen Charlotte's Ball the previous year, men were in short supply. Most were serving overseas, and the few who were left were either schoolboys or in reserved occupations like medicine, law or the church.

On Saturday 2 September, she made up a theatre party of five: Stella and me, two schoolboys – Michael Goulder, an Etonian tug,[18] and Dougal Kerr, a sixteen-year-old – and, as the third male, a medical student, one of the rare breed in a 'reserved occupation', whom Violet had winkled out. This is the twenty-two-year-old Peter Dallas Ross, who lives in the village. He is in his final year at Bart's medical school and comes home for weekends. He is tall, six foot three, and good-looking. From Violet's house we whizz down the hill to Windsor theatre on our bikes – there is no other way of getting about – and push them back again for supper and dancing to the gramophone. Peter is an excellent dancer, and, unsurprisingly, much sought after. I note in my diary, 'He has been to Charlotte's <u>masses</u> of times.' The following day I add, 'He is the first youngster in Englefield Green who does not repel me.'

* * *

One who did repel me was the unpleasant little SO. He did everything possible to make life difficult and refused to allow me to take a draft to Yarmouth in the Isle of Wight. Like Mr Montagu, he claimed that I 'cannot be spared.' His mistress, Pat Wyatt, was excused all the difficult jobs, and the Signal Wrens drew up a petition to remove him.

Most of the girls had boyfriends and I felt that I was missing out. Like nearly all my friends who had been to single-sex schools, I was naïve to the point of lunacy. One of them said that, before joining the Wrens, she always thought of a building site whenever she heard the word 'erection'. And so it was with no sense of foreboding that I arranged to get myself confirmed.

It is a November afternoon. I am sitting in a small cabin in HMS *Marshal Soult*. The naval padre is overweight, with thick pebble glasses and moist fleshy lips. The atmosphere is claustrophobic. He begins by asking me whether I wish to be prepared 'according to the prayer book' or 'according to life'. Foolishly, I choose the latter. His conversation, it seems to me, has nothing to do with getting confirmed. His breathing becomes faster and more laboured. He starts to ask me intimate questions about my private life and boyfriends. He tells me all sorts of things of which I have never heard and makes lewd suggestions about pencils. He puts his podgy hand on my breast. I think to myself that I must get out of here, but it is difficult – he is an officer and I am only a Wren. The conversation continues in this vein for about an hour until I make an excuse to leave. His last words are, 'Remember that this is a sacred conversation between these four walls and God. It must not be repeated to anyone else.'

Fortunately, my commanding officer, Second Officer Montenaro, was a sensible, sophisticated married woman. She was horrified when I told her what had happened. She advised me not to report him to the captain as it would only be my word against his. If it came to a court martial, I would find the whole thing distasteful and embarrassing. He would deny everything. She had a quiet word with the captain. A few weeks later, I heard that the padre had been posted overseas.

For those of us from sheltered homes, life in His Majesty's Navy was a revelation. I went everywhere on my bike. Riding through the blacked-out dockyard, skidding round the deep dry-docks, returning to quarters or going on duty, I learned much about life. There were constant obstacles to be avoided – sailors peeing against bulkheads or vomiting into the dry docks after a drunken night out. There was much good-natured banter directed at Wrens and one learned to be quick at repartee.[19] Because of my size, I was called 'shortie' or 'half-pint'.

Apart from work, my thoughts revolved around Peter Dallas Ross – quite the most attractive man I had yet met. Although he took my telephone number in September, I thought I was unlikely to hear from him. I was shy and backward, unlike Stella who fizzed in the company of men. My mother told me I had no sex appeal and that I should try to be more vivacious – which didn't help.

On Christmas morning, I was on watch in the SD office, where there was much merriment. One or two sailors, very drunk, decided to give us Christmas kisses. When I saw their slobbery, beery mouths pressed hard against the lips of the other Wrens, who seemed to enjoy it, I decided that I would have none of it and was considered very 'stuck-up'.

By this time, I had become disenchanted with the antics of my boss and his flame-haired mistress, and put in for a coding course. On Boxing Day I was suddenly told that it had come through and that I had been given seven days' immediate leave. I packed in a whirl and caught the train home. There was no time to tell my mother – she was spending Christmas with the Prestons in Canterbury – and so I let myself in to an empty Orchard Cottage. As usual, the Brookes were my salvation, and they gave me supper. Stella wanted to know every detail of my love life, and, when I confessed there was little to tell, persuaded me to ring Peter Dallas Ross, who was home for Christmas.

I am not as forward as Stella, and, rather against my will, decide to ring him the next morning. In great trepidation and shivering with apprehension, I dial Egham 126. His mother answers, and it is some time before Peter comes to the telephone. (I discovered later that I had dragged him out of bed at 10.30.) I tell him that I am feeling very lonely and suggest we go to the flicks. He jumps at the idea, says he is 'bored to tears', and comes round to fetch me shortly afterwards. We bike to Windsor where we have drinks (gin and lime) at the White Hart, followed by lunch at the Old House and a film, *Dead End*, in Slough. The following evening we go dancing in Windsor, again by bike. Taxis are impossible to find. The dance at the Old House is great fun – 'mostly the Windsor elite, all in long dinner dresses, sparkling with diamonds'. I have had to wear a short dress as we are on bikes. We enjoy each other's company, though I note that 'bikes are not conducive to love.' He says it is the nicest evening he has ever spent in Englefield Green. He also tells me that he has 'a very great friend in the Wrens', which somewhat dampens my elation.

On New Year's Eve, he invites me to a medical students' party in London. I catch the 15.40 train up to Waterloo, where he is waiting. After dining at the Hong Kong Chinese restaurant in Shaftesbury Avenue, we go on to the party in Ladbroke Grove. Drink flows. We dance and sing rowdy songs – 'My Brother Sylveste' and 'Abdul, the Bulbul Amir'. During 'Lily of Laguna', where it goes 'I know she loves me', our eyes meet. I hope, and hope so much, that he does. At midnight, when we all sing 'Auld Lang Syne', he kisses me on the lips under the mistletoe. Everyone else pecked my cheek. At 02.30, we leave the party to walk the mile or so back to his flat in Maida Vale. As we stroll along the bank of the canal in the moonlight, I long to be gathered into his arms, but the shadow of the 'very great friend in the Wrens' intervenes. I am young and impressionable; he is much too honourable a chap to raise my hopes. We go chastely to bed.[20] I have never had such a magical evening and note 'am falling rapidly'. The new year has begun.

* * *

On Wednesday 3 January 1945, I arrived at the Royal Naval Signal School, HMS *Cabbala*, a motley collection of tin huts about four miles north of Warrington. Lancashire was a part of the country that I did not know, and first impressions were of a dreary, northern landscape, inhabited by dreary, colourless people.

It had taken all day to travel by train from Portsmouth, via Euston, and after arriving at Warrington at 17.30 I reached *Cabbala* two hours later, in pitch darkness. I found the camp very pusser, a naval word meaning that everything had to be done 'Shipshape and Bristol Fashion', to the nth degree. The camp was mixed, and we were here for six weeks. The course did not start until Monday, so the first thing on Thursday morning was the inevitable head inspection. Lectures on gas and respirator drill followed. We had to wear our gasmasks for half an hour every week while we were working, which was claustrophobic. I shared a cabin with Audrey Wallin, who lived in Northampton. Saturday afternoon was free and Audrey (whom I describe as 'a very sweet girl')[21] and I hitched a lift into Liverpool, to see the film *Love Story*.

My fellow-Wrens on the coding course at HMS *Cabbala*, Warrington, 1945. I am sitting, second left; Audrey Wallin, my cabin-mate, is standing on the right of the back row; the Petty Officer Instructor is seated in the centre of the front row.

January 1945 was exceptionally cold, and on one day we had twenty-four degrees of frost, i.e. the temperature dropped to eight degrees Fahrenheit.[22] Although our classrooms, which were no more than glorified tin huts, were heated by coke stoves, fed by strapping sailors every few hours, my chilblains soon started again, and were torture.

Apart from work, which was hard and relentless, there was little to do. Sometimes we caught the 'liberty boat' (a naval lorry) or hitched lifts into Manchester or Wigan to dance. I met a few reasonable young men, mostly in the RAF, but I had given my heart to Peter Dallas Ross, and so was not interested.

At the end of six weeks, we had our final exams. We had learned a variety of naval codes, some of them complicated. I was relieved to find I had passed the practical with 89 per cent and had come top of the theory with 95 per cent. Out of the twenty-three Wrens on our course, thirteen had failed. Two days later, I was drafted to the holding depot at Rochester, in the Nore Command.

Naval holding depots were places where Wrens were held while the powers-that-be thought what to do with us. I did not know Rochester, and we were housed in the Deanery, an old ivy-clad Georgian house overlooking the Medway. There was little to do except scrub floors and clean lavatories, and I was bored. After four weeks of housework, the three remaining coders who had been drafted with me went to see the First Officer. We explained that we were forgetting everything we had learned, so she arranged for us to go up to C-in-C's office to get some practice. I noted that 'I love coding.'

Like all the women's services, the Wrens attracted a certain type of female. One of these Eton-cropped characters, First Officer Fletcher, put her head round the door and yelled, 'Anyone for the GAS BUGGY?' This was the naval lorry in which we travelled to C-in-C's headquarters. I can still remember the sound of her voice.

After I had been in Rochester for six weeks, volunteers were requested for the Orkneys. I realised that my feelings for Peter were only infatuation, and, in an effort to erase him from my heart, decided to go as far away as possible.

On 9 April, I was at home for a few days' leave when I got a wire saying that a draft for the Orkneys had come through and that an immediate reply was required. Although I was seeing Peter the next day, I decided to be strong-minded and caught the next train back to Rochester.

The following day, I rose at 06.00 to begin the thirty-hour journey to Scapa Flow. Leaving Euston at 10.05, the train reached Perth at 20.30. A Canadian soldier took me out for a drink and dinner. Afterwards, all the women were put in a separate train and not allowed to travel with men unless one was 'man and wife'. They took great care of our virtue.

* * *

After a fitful night, sleeping uneasily sitting up, I awoke to the sight of a Scottish dawn. There was nothing to see except mile upon mile of moorland. No sound but the distant bleating of sheep. I had never been so far north before. About 08.00 we reached Thurso where we were taken to the Wrennery for a breakfast of sausage and fried eggs – a treat rare enough to be noted in my diary. At 10.30 we boarded the ship which took us to the Orkneys. The Pentland Firth, which divides the islands from the mainland, is notoriously rough – a thrashing maelstrom where seven channels meet. To my surprise, I was not sick and we arrived at Lyness, the naval base, at 14.30. A small drifter took us from the ship to the quay. Here agility and a head for heights were needed as we leapt across a heaving void to climb two dozen iron rungs to the top.

After the glorious scenery of northern Scotland, Lyness was a disappointment. Nothing to see but rows of tin huts with huge hills in the distance – no trees or hedges in sight. This was the headquarters of Commander-in-Chief Home Fleet – the nerve centre of Northern Command. There were six thousand men and six hundred Wrens to look after them. In Scapa Flow, to the north, dozens of iron-grey battleships, cruisers and destroyers rode at anchor – the biggest of all was HMS *Rodney* in which C-in-C Home Fleet flew his flag.

Captain's Rounds,[23] visits to the sick bay and dentist, and interviews took up most of the first day. The dormitories were huge, with thirty Wrens in each. One of my shipmates was Nancy Howard, a tall *jolie laide* of twenty-four, whom I had met in Chatham.[24] Well connected – a scion of Castle Howard – she and I became close friends. After being on watch, we explored the island together by bike and hired a sailing boat from two fishermen. The water was treacherous – squalls can spring up without warning. On our first trip, we nearly capsized, but fortunately the owners were with us and we were rescued by a motor boat. Much of our time was spent in the YWCA hut,[25] where hot coffee and scrambled eggs were dispensed by the large and friendly Primula Oliphant, known as Prim.

It was clear to all of us that the war in Europe was almost over. On 3 May I noted that 'Berlin has fallen, and Italy surrendered.'

126

Jill McNaughton WRNS,
in 1945, aged nineteen.

The next day, 'Marvellous news – whole of NW Germany, Denmark, Holland surrendered. Rangoon fallen. Should think the war will be over any day now.'

We did not have long to wait. On 7 May we heard 'The War with Germany is over!!!' Churchill spoke to the nation at 15.00 but in subdued rather than jubilant tones, reminding us that we still had to beat the Japanese. Tuesday 8 May was declared V-E Day[26] and the whole of Scapa Flow went mad. Ships' hooters and sirens went off all day, and at midnight we watched rockets being let off from Wee Fea (our signal station on the top of the hill).

Almost immediately the base began to wind down. On 22 May, HMS *Rodney* sailed for Rosyth. An air of emptiness and nostalgia pervaded us as more Wrens departed. Soon there were very few coders left. But the war in the Far East was still raging, and volunteers were asked for overseas. I asked my mother's permission, which she gave, but so reluctantly that I knew I could not go. Some of my friends said that I should not be tied to her apron strings, and so, after a leave at home, I decided to apply.

There were still ships in the Flow,[27] and on 23 June Prim Oliphant arranged a party at the Officers' Club at which were five young officers from the destroyer HMS *Comet*. One of them, Peter Spicer, I found distinctly attractive, and I now realised that my feelings for Peter Dallas Ross were not very deep.

There was less and less to do on watch, and boredom soon set in. By 20 July, I was one of only three coders remaining. Six days later, as the results of the general election were declared, I 'heard the appalling news on the wireless that Labour have got in with a big majority of 300 or more over 100 odd Conservatives! Everyone will be nationalised now and England won't be worth living in.' The Navy was shocked that Churchill, who had led us to victory, was cast out by the masses.

On 28 July, the Officers' Club closed for good. Scapa Flow was winding down. The following day, I was in a hockey team which played one of the last remaining destroyers, HMS *Onslow*. It was great fun. They asked us again, three days later, to be followed by a party on board. Although First Officer withheld her permission, we decided to go 'unofficially' (rather risky if we had been caught). *Onslow* had just returned from Copenhagen, and drink flowed. I am appalled to read how much I drank: 'I started off with half a Schnapps, washed down with some beer, then a cherry brandy, two crème de menthe, another cherry brandy, gin and orange, then a gin and lime.' My head was quite unused to this amount of drink, but I was looked after by the Asdic[28] Officer, Lieutenant Ian Jamieson,[29] who refused (quite rightly) to let me have a second glass of schnapps. *Onslow* was part of the 17th Destroyer Flotilla, D.17, and its No. 1, Ken Cradock-Hartopp, was an amusing character with come-to-bed eyes, who sang bawdy songs which he accompanied on his guitar. Ian and I danced amorously to 'I'm beginning to see the light', and the party did not end until 00.30.

Little by little, the ships left the Flow and there was less for us to do. I was interviewed by an overseas board for a posting to Ceylon or Australia, but it was clear that the war was almost over. On 10

August, I wrote in block capitals: 'UNCONFIRMED REPORTS THAT JAPAN HAS ACCEPTED THE POTSDAM SURRENDER TERMS.' Despite the jubilation, there was the nagging fear of what the future held. For over a year, I had been coddled and protected by the Navy, and the thought of going into an unknown world was frightening. Like most of my friends, I was only a secretary.

* * *

On 17 August, I and one or two others left Scapa Flow for good. I was sorry to leave – the Flow had been an experience, a new world, and the islands held much remote beauty. We crossed the Pentland Firth and caught the 20.00 train from Thurso to Perth, where we arrived at 05.15.

Pittencrieff Holding Depot in Dunfermline was a depressing place, made worse by the fact that there was little to do except scrub the floors and lavatories. After two days, I was delighted to hear that I was being lent to the Commander-in-Chief at Pitreavie, Rosyth on an urgent draft.

The signals network for C-in-C Rosyth was housed underground in a vast warren of offices and passages, lit by curious strip lighting which turned everything a bright yellow/green, including the scrambled eggs we made on night duty. This time we were in three watches: 19.00–00.00 one day, 13.00–19.00 the next, followed by 07.00–13.00 on the third day with a 19.00–00.00 watch the same evening. It was quite tiring, with little chance to recharge batteries in between. However, the monotony of the work – typing and duplicating signals with an old Ormig machine – was relieved by the fact that several of my Scapa Flow chums were there. I was delighted to find Elizabeth Cumming in my cabin, and we became close friends. She had (and has) a lovely sense of humour and we spent a lot of time laughing.[30]

One evening, Liz arrived back in quarters after having been to a smart luncheon party given by General Sir Neil Ritchie, the GOC Scotland,[31] at Edinburgh Castle. 'I've met the most divine man,' she gasped. I shall never forget the catch in her voice. A week or so later, when she and I went to the flicks in Edinburgh, a message for

'Wren Cumming' to go to the manager's office was flashed on to the screen. When she returned, she told me that Angus Irwin, the young man in question, had asked her out that evening. Angus, a Captain in the Black Watch, was General Ritchie's aide-de-camp. Tall and craggy, with reddish hair, and a gifted artist, he had been a prisoner in Germany. By 11 November they were engaged to be married. She was nineteen, he nine years older. I thought she was extremely young to make such a bold decision.

One day, I picked up *The Times* to read of Peter Dallas Ross' engagement to Mary Elizabeth Hume Wright, WRNS. I was numb with shock, but after a night's sleep realised that my feelings were mainly hurt pride. There had never been anything very serious between us.

On 9 November, I was surprised to be rung up by Ian Jamieson. His ship was in Glasgow, and he had been trying to find me all over Scotland. We arranged to meet in Edinburgh the following day. After lunching at the North British, we dined and danced and went to a show. I was still raw from my supposed rejection by Peter[32] and could not respond. Immature for my age, I judged all men by their looks and failed to see the gold within. It would be another ten years before I did so.

The Navy filled our time with lectures to prepare us, like fledgling birds, for the wider world: local government, the falling birth rate, current affairs, home-making – all good, worthy objectives. Part of this so-called 'citizenship course' involved going to the Edinburgh Royal Infirmary, where we saw an operation on the base of the spine. I noted that it was 'very interesting'. Another day, we were lent to Kirkcaldy General Hospital where we wore green overalls with veils and were addressed as 'nurse'. We started off in the children's ward and were then transferred to 'females', where I spent the time emptying bedpans and Pam Wilson had to wash 'nauseating bandages'.

Another close friendship from Rosyth was with Mary Bovill. She and I found we were kindred spirits and we have remained lifelong friends. She was one of three sisters[33] whose family had lived in Shropshire for generations. Two years earlier, her father, a

Master of Foxhounds, had shot himself while mentally unbalanced. She and her mother were in touch with him through a medium and he was said to be 'very happy'. A deeply spiritual girl, of great serenity, she introduced me to philosophy and to many unusual books. Under her guidance I read Bertrand Russell's *History of Western Philosophy* and Rom Landau's *God is my Adventure*, which made a deep impression.[34] I began to appreciate poetry and discovered Eliot, Auden and Rupert Brooke.

Mary is a darling girl, but accident prone. She had joined the Wrens straight out of school, at the age of eighteen. After a secretarial course at Queen's, Englefield Green (where I had been), she had a modicum of shorthand and typing skills. Arriving at Donibristle, a Naval Air station in Scotland, she was made an armourer, the lowest form of technical support (the highest being an electrician). Owing to a clerical error, she found herself the only woman in a squad of men, all fairly rough Glaswegians, who spoke a vernacular she found almost impossible to understand. It never

Mary Bovill WRNS, another lifelong friend, in 1945, aged nineteen.

occurred to her, being young and unsophisticated, that she should not have been in this job. She lived by night in the Wrennery, and by day she was collected by liberty boat and transported to the aircraft hangar where she was supposed to work as an armourer, stripping and cleaning the guns.

The men, headed by a belligerent RAF sergeant, resented this cuckoo in the nest. They were obliged to watch their language in front of this flower of English maidenhood and used every excuse to get her out of their way. On one occasion, she was given a bottle and told to get some 'red oil for the port light'. This, being non-existent, naturally took her some time, but she dutifully went her way round the camp, searching for this elusive commodity, and managed to use up most of the day. Another time, she was told to find 'an aircraft screw',[35] and was given a matchbox to put it in. The men fell about laughing as they regaled their chums with ever-more unlikely tasks that they thought up to get rid of their unwelcome guest. The final indignity came when she was told to go to the Captain of the Air Station and ask for 'a long weight'. Having in mind the sort of weight that hangs from a grandfather clock, she had no idea that her leg was being pulled, hard. Dutifully, she knocked on the door of the Commanding Officer's sanctum, and asked for 'a long weight', as she had been told to do. The Captain, a kindly man, told her to sit down and chatted to her for some time. After an interval, Mary began to wonder how much longer he would keep her in polite conversation and asked when he was going to give her the item she had requested. 'Well, my dear,' he replied, 'you've been here for over twenty minutes, I think you've waited long enough.'

After this, the Captain must have made enquiries and the 'clerical error' was discovered.

After six months or so, an unhappy Mary returned home to her mother on leave. She was not enjoying life as a Wren. Her mother took one look at her and decided that something must be done. She did not wish her daughter to be discharged from the Service, for then she would have to have her at home without a ration book, which would be a strain on the housekeeping.

Mrs Bovill, an eccentric and lively woman, took out her green ink and wrote to the Chief Wren on a postcard, her usual mode of communication: 'You have returned my daughter to me, but not in the state in which I sent her. <u>What are you going to do about it?</u>'

When Wren Bovill returned to camp, she was sent for. The Chief Wren Officer interrogated her. 'Well, Bovill, what have you got to say for yourself?' As Mary had absolutely no idea what she was supposed to have done, she hung her head, and mumbled that she did not know. Immediate action followed. She was told to pack her things that very afternoon, and transport arrived to take her to 'the holding depot'. When she asked what a holding depot was, she was told it was where Wrens were held. She arrived in a bleak building in Dunfermline, formerly a girls' school. After six weeks in the company of the lowest of the low, mainly Glaswegian cooks and stewards of ill repute, spending her days scrubbing floors, she began to wonder what on earth she was doing there.

One day, a Wren officer who had known her earlier in her career, arrived to look round the place. 'Bovill,' she exclaimed, 'what on <u>earth</u> are <u>you</u> doing here?' Mary replied that she had absolutely no idea. The officer sent for her file and was amazed to discover that Wren Bovill was pregnant. She was to remain in the depot for four months, until her pregnancy was confirmed. No medical examination had taken place, and senior officers had jumped to one conclusion when they received her mother's cryptic card. The whole thing was fallacious and has shades of my own experience at Cheltenham. You were guilty until proved innocent.

After her release, with little or no apology, her Aunt Adela[36] heard of the matter. Aunt Adela was a powerful lady, well used to the corridors of power, and had the ear of the Chief Wren herself, the indomitable Dame Vera Laughton Matthews. Wheels were set in motion and an enquiry demanded as to why her niece had endured this ignominy. A slight apology followed, but nothing else happened.

* * *

Early in January 1946, after ten weeks in Dunfermline, I was drafted to HMS *Europa*, a large demobilisation centre for men, in Lowestoft. Four of us travelled overnight from Edinburgh, sitting upright in a third-class carriage. The journey was made unpleasant by a drunk soldier who made a dead set at me. When I resisted, he became abusive. At Newcastle, I got out of the train and fetched the Military Police, who removed him. In those days, women, particularly Wrens in uniform, were looked after most paternally.

Everyone was being demobbed, and one of the first to go was my father. At the outbreak of war, he had been too old to rejoin his old regiment, The Black Watch, and was drafted, with others of his age, to the Pioneer Corps. However uninspiring it may have been, for him it was better than nothing. Now, at the age of fifty-four, he was once again adrift on the open sea, lacking the friends and support that the army had provided. There was no way that my mother was going to 'take him back', as she put it. It was left to me, the only remaining child, to hold the peace between them, and to do what I could to make up to him for the loss of Peggy, something I could never hope to achieve. There was no rapport between us, which I found a great sadness. Like Stewart with his son, he denigrated me and made constant references to other people's much more marvellous children. I found him hypocritical and sarcastic. 'He must always know better and be better than anybody else and is continually belittling other people's opinions.' In hindsight, this was probably a form of inferiority derived from the fact that he, with all his gifts, had achieved so little. Good looks and charm were not enough. He found a job at the Board of Trade and lived in a dismal bed-sitting room where I visited him and found it 'rather sordid'.

Early in February, just before a weekend leave, I received a 'rather alarming' letter from my uncle Stewart, saying that my father had had a stroke. Stewart implied, very strongly, that if my father did not progress I would have to get compassionate leave and come to 'deal with the situation'. Once more, I was pig in the middle, trying to sort out the muddled affairs of my parents. My mother and I went to the Hampstead nursing home where he was recovering, and found him better than we had expected from

Stewart's dismal report. He seemed to be more or less normal, apart from mild paralysis of his left arm and leg, which was beginning to mend.

Stewart was in much the same position as I was. Since the death of my grandparents, he had taken upon himself the burden of dealing with all the 'family affairs'. His financial acumen as a chartered accountant was much in demand. In addition, he felt responsible for his feckless elder brother. During all these years, when my parents were rootless, Stewart and Enid at Stansted provided a bulwark of support. It was therefore natural that, when my father was well enough, he should go to Roycot to convalesce. He had nowhere else to go. He suggested that I should apply for compassionate leave so that I could also go and help.

The situation was exacerbated by my mother's health. Now fifty-two, she was suffering from acute sciatica and she, too, wanted my support. I began to feel the overwhelming burden of being an only child. Throughout the war, she had been conducting an amorous correspondence with one of my father's Canadian friends – someone she had not seen for twenty years or more. Each post, she waited for his passionate letters, and her spirits climbed or sank according to their contents. They were both feeding on long-ago memories and were doomed to disappointment when reality arrived. My request for a month's leave was granted, and I divided my time between my parents.

I was surprised, one morning, to get a letter from Ian Jamieson, asking me to go out with him in London. I could not think where to stay until my mother suggested Roland, now the 3rd Baron Airedale. He and his second wife, Christabel, lived in a handsome house in Chelsea Square, and they kindly put me up for the night.

Well heeled and well connected, Ian was a career naval officer. Later he became Captain of Dartmouth and a Rear-Admiral. Now twenty-six, he had earned the Distinguished Service Order in an action in which he lost the tops of two fingers. He was an exceptionally nice guy. But, as always, I could not see beyond the surface. He had his own car, and we started the evening at the theatre, seeing Margaretta Scott in *The Hasty Heart*. Later we dined at La Belle

Etoile, a well-known Soho restaurant. Although Ian belonged to both Ciro's and the Orchid Room, he took me to the Four Hundred, now the most fashionable nightclub in London. Between us we consumed a bottle of gin, and danced amorously. But there was no spark on my side, and he must have found it a disappointing evening. Unsurprisingly, I had a hangover next day.

When my parents were both on an even keel once more, I returned to Lowestoft after an absence of six weeks. HMS *Europa* was non-operational and the Signal Office was tiny, with only two on watch at a time. It was a time of slow easing down.

This was not a part of England I knew well, except for the holidays spent with Nanny at Wenhaston and Aunt Sylvia at Benhall, who asked me to visit them. One Saturday, I caught the train from Lowestoft to Saxmundham, changing at Beccles, a journey that took an hour and a quarter. Halstead and Sylvia met me on the platform and took me off to the Rectory for lunch. Like her father, Sylvia was very deaf. This made her seem juvenile and gave her the reputation of being slightly mad – her sisters had little compassion. She repeated over and over again how nice it was to see me, accompanied by a high-pitched cackle. They were very kind, but neither had much sense of humour. Living with Sylvia must have been a strain for Halstead – she was really quite childish. Few of the Kitson husbands had chosen well: the cachet was all.

The monotony of the last couple of months, and the boredom of winding down, were enlivened by Jinny Wyllie's sister Suzanne, who was working at Lowestoft Hospital as a physiotherapist. She was huge fun, and we became firm friends, spending much time together. Although only twenty-one, she looked older and had a veneer of sophistication that I lacked. Blonde and beautiful, she had fallen in love with the house surgeon at the hospital, an attractive Irishman called Stephen Casey.[37]

The time when I would leave the Navy for good loomed ever nearer, and I had no idea what I was going to do. On my last leave, I had found the parochial world of Englefield Green claustrophobic. My mother and I seemed to have drifted apart, and she told me that I had become hard and unfeeling. I had simply grown up.

Notes

1. Now Jinny Lowe.
2. The probationer Wrens were divided into four Divisions, Nelson, Anson, Collingwood and Howe, named after famous admirals.
3. Signal Distribution Office.
4. Motor Transport.
5. Bedrooms, floors and lavatories.
6. Quotation from my diary. All unattributed quotations are from that source.
7. A voluntary movement started during the First World War by the Reverend 'Tubby' Clayton, an army chaplain, giving friendship and spiritual help to servicemen and women.
8. Distributed by the Supply Branch or 'Pussers' (naval slang for pursers and also used adjectivally – see page 123).
9. This was Julia Bovill, Mary's sister (see page 131), who had plenty of money.
10. Lord Montagu of Beaulieu started the famous Motor Museum.
11. Pronounced 'cassoons'.
12. A 'wavy' ring denoted that he was a temporary officer, Royal Naval Volunteer Reserve (RNVR), rather than Royal Navy.
13. Nicholas Monsarrat described the type perfectly in *The Cruel Sea*.
14. British Yard Minesweepers and Motor Minesweepers.
15. A type of duplicator, similar to a Gestetner, which, by using spirit, produced copies of documents. The master copy, which could be typed or handwritten, was fastened to a drum; when you turned a handle, copies churned out in violet ink.
16. See pages 91 and 140.
17. Food rationing began in 1940. The weekly ration for one person was one egg, one ounce butter, two ounces cooking fat, two ounces margarine, two ounces tea, eight ounces sugar, one ounce cheese, four ounces bacon and ham, and meat to the value of one shilling and two pence.
18. Scholar.
19. In these 'politically correct' days, this would be called 'verbal sexual abuse'.
20. He lent me his bedroom and slept in the passage.
21. One evening, I had a long chat with Audrey about sex. I noted 'she is most terribly innocent at 23, she feels marriage is repulsive and not to be talked about.' She went on to marry the brilliant Peter White, afterwards my husband's boss in the Admiralty, one of the sexiest men in the Navy. As Admiral Sir Peter White, a widower of seventy-nine, he made a pass at me in September 1998 (i.e. he waited exactly a year after Peter died, to ask me to marry him, a proposal I firmly turned down).
22. About -16° C.
23. The Captain's daily inspection.
24. She later married Peter Hattersley, a Gunner officer, whose photograph remained by her bed.
25. Young Women's Christian Association
26. Victory in Europe Day
27. The huge bay between the small islands where the Home Fleet was anchored.

[28] Asdic, later known as sonar, was a secret device for using sound waves to locate submerged submarines. It was named after the Anti-Submarine Detection Investigation Committee. The sonic waves made a 'ping' when they found a target, and Asdic officers were invariably known as 'Ping'.

[29] I didn't then know that Ian played hockey for Scotland.

[30] Her father, Ronald Cumming, was chairman of the Distillers Company from 1963 to 1967 and was knighted in 1965. Her mother, Mary Hendrie, was a delightful Canadian. Liz and I have remained close friends.

[31] General Officer Commanding.

[32] Although he had given me absolutely no encouragement.

[33] Her elder sister, Julia, was an SDO watchkeeper Wren in Plymouth with Jinny Wyllie and they became lifelong friends. Jinny later became a Plotter and Julia an MT driver. (See note 9.)

[34] I still have my book list, started in 1936, so can check the titles.

[35] An aircraft propeller.

[36] Viscountess Broome, widow of the son of the second Earl Kitchener of Khartoum and of Broome, brother of the first Earl, the Field Marshal hero of the Great War (of 'your country needs you' fame), who was unmarried.

[37] They married in 1948 and emigrated to Canada. I met her youngest daughter, with Jinny, in 2006.

Jill McNaughton,
Wren Coder,
Lowestoft, April 1946,
aged twenty.

Additional Notes on Volume One

Since writing Volume 1, I have discovered more about my great-grandfather's second wife, Mary Laura Fisher Smith. She left him suddenly in 1888 after only seven years of marriage, having borne him two children, Roland, in 1882, and Olive, in 1887. According to Kitson family lore,[1] one of the Barrans, a prominent Leeds textile family and leading Liberals, was said to be Olive's father. Apparently, Sir James, having been tipped off and returning unexpectedly to Gledhow Hall, caught her in bed with her lover. Unsurprisingly, this precipitated her flight. She was pensioned off, but Sir James did not divorce her, thus precluding her remarriage. It was said that she had an illegitimate son living in Buenos Aires.[2] It is perhaps ironic that she died as 'Lady Airedale' and that it was her son, Roland, who inherited the title as the Third Baron. Mary Laura came from a seriously rich family – her great-grandfather, Thomas Smith, was said to be the second richest man in Staffordshire, after the Earl of Dudley. Her uncle, Frederick Shenstone, a banker, was High Sheriff of East Sussex in 1886; her four brothers were barristers and doctors.[3] Thus her background would explain my grandfather's remark to his sister in 1887 that 'Her ladyship is a fiend... an example of what a high marriage leads to without love.'[4]

I failed to thank three people who helped me greatly with Volume One. First, Eileen Cox, local historian in Dunkeld, Perthshire, who pointed me towards the Duke of Atholl's memoir[5] in which is recounted the story of Donald Keir. Second, Forbes Taylor, who found for me the impressive print of the McNaughton Highlander which graced the jacket. And last, but by no means least, my old friend Peter Dallas Ross, of Blairgowrie, Perthshire, who trudged with me along the grassy course of the Dundee–Newtyle Railway on which my great-grandfather James had worked. Peter also did much devilling for me in local libraries. To all three, my most grateful thanks.

Notes

[1] Recounted by Dr David Boswell in his D.Phil thesis *The Kitsons and the Arts*, Institute for Advanced Architectural Studies, University of York, 1996.

[2] See page 59 of *Call Back Yesterday*, volume 1 of these memoirs.

[3] Information from Gloria Hargreaves, an Australian correspondent who is a Smith descendant.

[4] Albert to Emily, November 1887. West Yorkshire Archives. WYL 893/22.

[5] Atholl, 7th Duke of, *Chronicles of the Atholl and Tullibardine Families*, 5 volumes, Ballantyne Press, Edinburgh, 1908.

Cassilis House, Ayrshire, the childhood home of Hilary Wyllie (*née* Strain).

Index